Techniques of Photographing
WOMEN

by Peter Barry

CHARTWELL
BOOKS, INC.

CONTENTS

Introduction

Whether you want to take up girl photography as a profession or you simply wish to photograph your wife, girlfriend or the girl next door, the object of this book is to explain how to go about it. It will, hopefully, save you time, film and, maybe, embarrassment. While the subject of equipment – cameras, lenses, films and filters – will be dealt with, and is important, it is equally important to gain an understanding of the subject; what is expected of the photograph, the problems – if any – in photographing the model, the best way to light her and enhance her best features while concealing those that are not so good; how to portray her as either soft, romantic and feminine or sensuous and aggressive. How, when lighting her, to bring life and vitality to her eyes, make her mouth look inviting, her legs appear long even when they are not; how to make her look slimmer or fuller-figured; how to make her skin look smoother, softer, browner and her hair shinier. The list of what can be accomplished is almost endless,

and it will be explained in the chapters and sections that follow.

Photographing girls as a profession can be considered under several different and distinct headings, such as editorial fashion, catalogue, advertising, glamour and erotic. Each of these different groupings requires a difference in approach, both in relation to the photography and to the model. It follows, therefore, that if you are working in a professional manner on the various groups you must have the ability to change both your attitude and working methods in each case. There is, for instance, a considerable difference between working on a fashion assignment, where the clothes are obviously the main consideration, and a calendar featuring girls, where everything must be subordinate to the feeling of glamour, and the girls, and how good they look, must be the photographer's prime concern.

Whatever your reasons for deciding to photograph girls, it is essential – as, indeed, it is for any other subject – that you are

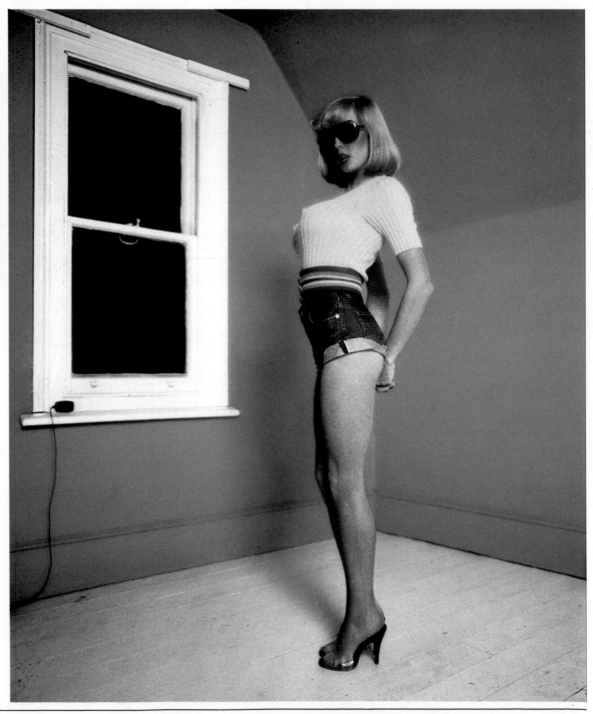

Creation of a mood, whether it be frivolous, serious or whatever, is an important part of the photographer's job. The make-up, the elaborate hair styling–for which a hair stylist would, in this particular case, be a must–suggested the dark, sophisticated atmosphere of the shot above in which the only strong colour accent is the model's lipstick. The veil, hat and jewellery serve to emphasise the mood and do not compete with, or detract from, the impact of the picture. (Hasselblad).

Although all the ingredients of the picture right are perfectly ordinary–a model standing in the corner of a plain room with a window–the choice of pose, the combination of strong colours, the incongruity of the sunglasses, together with the model's expression, create an air of unreality. (Hasselblad)

Black has been used to particularly telling effect in both the pictures above. The photographer draped black plastic over a support above left and used it to emphasise the model's legs. For the fashion shot above an apparently plain background was used but when this—and the model—were lit by a single electronic flash, the texture of the background became very apparent. This has added interest to the picture but has still allowed the clothing—the real subject of the session—to remain dominant. The hair has also been styled in keeping with the outfit but is not so startling as to be a distraction.

The symmetry of the head-on shot featuring the motor cycle left has been echoed by the symmetrical pose, broken only by the inclination of the model's head. (All pictures this page: Hasselblad cameras)

Introduction

totally familiar with your equipment. Given this, you can then start to study your subject. As with any other subject, you will need to examine a face or body carefully to determine the best features and angles. Watch how the light – both in strength and direction – affects your subject; softening or harshening, improving or harming. Remember that moving the camera position up or down even an inch or two can make all the difference.

Once you start actually taking pictures you must try to learn from each one, endeavouring to improve each time you press the shutter release. This will only come about if you take lots of pictures and lose any fear you may have of using too much film.

Top lighting was used right *to accentuate the startling hairstyle in a shot taken for a Japanese hair stylist's publicity.*

Very carefully applied make-up, for an advertisement for a cosmetic company, was lit top right *with very soft, even lighting to emphasise its delicate subtlety.*

Shot for Gina Fratini dresses, the uncompromising picture below right *was arranged to underline the idea of women who know exactly what they want and how they wish to project themselves.*

The delicately beautiful picture of Joni above *shows how expert lighting and one simple piece of drapery can be used to considerable effect.*

Antigua, in the West Indies, was the chosen setting for an assignment for Silhouette swimwear. The three models were posed in the shade to allow the even lighting. (Picture above: Mamiya RB67, all others: Hasselblad cameras)

The Models

The term 'model' usually conjures up a picture of a tall, willowy girl with a less than shapely figure, a cool, disdainful look and a slightly bored air. In fact, models couldn't vary more from that image, and they come in all shapes, sizes and ages. Models are required for many different types of assignments: high fashion to catalogue fashion; advertising photography involving a beautiful girl sipping a cocktail against an exotic tropical sunset to a housewife dressed in an apron and sitting on a refrigerator surrounded by pots and pans; calendars featuring girls with voluptuous figures bursting out of tiny, contrived outfits to girls writhing in the sea, stretching their ultra-long legs tantalisingly toward the camera; girls who specialise in underwear and corsetry and who are shaped in such a way that they fill each garment to perfection – with never a crease or bump where there shouldn't be one; girls who are rather large and who specialise in outsize fashion for the fuller figure; product shots, where the main requirement is just a face with a really animated expression and an ability to register sheer joy, misery, worry, surprise, and so on. There are also girls who concentrate on a very narrow field of specialisation, such as leg shots for stockings and tights manufacturers, and, of course, hands; it is surprising just how much demand there is for girls with beautiful hands. Additionally, there are girls who are engaged for shots of feet, lips, eyes, hair etc. There may also be occasions when models are required to skate, water ski, horse ride, swim underwater or just light and smoke a cigarette.

Virtually all models work through agents. While a model is working on one job the agent can be arranging for another. The agent can inform clients about the model and her availability, and can recommend her as being suitable when a particular job comes up. Meetings between model and client can be arranged, either at the agency or at the client's premises. These meetings

Facing page. *Strong*
backgrounds used to complement the moods and ideas of the shots. The stippled background, top picture was painted with black gloss paint to provide the unusual reflective quality. For the picture bottom centre a plain coloured background was used but lights were directed onto it from either side to add interest, while the shot bottom left displays a different technique. Here, gloss paint was sprayed thickly at the top of the background and allowed to run, enhancing the rather macabre make-up and hair style.

One girl, three totally different *looks! A change of clothes, hairstyles, expression and lighting has completely transformed the demure miss above to the directly challenging woman top and the sophisticated and sensual model left.*
(All shots on these pages: Hasselblad cameras)

The Models

are known as 'go sees' or, in France, as 'rendezvous' and, during them, models can show their portfolio and leave a card on which between one and ten photographs are printed, either in black and white or colour. Included on the card will be the model's measurements, colour of eyes and hair, shoe size etc., plus any speciality that may be thought worth including, such as, in addition to those mentioned previously, acting experience or dancing ability.

It might be imagined that, at such meetings, the appearance and personality of the girl would be of paramount importance and yet some models turn up in drab outfits, wearing virtually no make-up and with greasy hair, and just sit there while their portfolio is examined, making no attempt to comment. Presumably they feel that it is their photogenic qualities that are being considered, and if they have a portfolio of beautiful pictures showing how they can be transformed, and how well they photograph, and the client understands this, then they may still be booked.

Another function of the agent is to protect the girls from undesirable clients – who may either have the wrong kind of work in mind, or be simply unable to pay the ever-increasing fees charged. Incidentally, modelling fees work in the following way: there is a basic fee, per hour, which may sometimes be lowered slightly for full day bookings, although this is usually negotiable. If she is engaged for editorial fashion work she is paid a set fee by the magazine which is much less than her normal rate, but as this is usually considered to be prestigious work it is accepted. If she will agree to topless modelling, when required, then she will expect about a third more than her normal fee, and nude work usually means an increase of half or even more, depending on how good and how much in demand she is. This may seem strange; being paid more for doing nude modelling than a fashion model who will be expected to bring with her a selection of accessories, such as hats, gloves, shoes, stockings, underwear and jewellery, all of which is expensive to keep up to date and heavy to drag around from studio to studio. On the other hand, there are fewer models willing – and suitable – to appear nude, so it comes down to a question of supply and demand.

On top of the basic fees there are extra charges if the photographs are used on showcards, posters, packaging and record covers – and these 'extra' fees can sometimes amount to a five hundred percent increase over the original!

For a photographic session, unless a make-up artist or hairdresser has been made available, a model is expected to arrive either fully made-up and ready to work, or fifteen minutes earlier than the time specified so that she can prepare herself. Unfortunately, however, this does not always happen and it is not

A photographer and model can work together without necessarily being friends. However, some kind of relationship has to be formed, if only to the point where respect for the photographer's ability and integrity is established on the one hand, and on the other, respect and understanding are afforded the model. Although a model may be very experienced, a visit to a new, to her, photographer whose work she may not know, carries with it all the natural *anxiety that most of us experience when starting a new job, and some time is required before both the model and the photographer feel at ease with each other. Again, although a model may have posed nude or semi-clothed many times before, this type of photography is, in itself, an intimate act and while one particular model may approach a session with a great deal of self-confidence, in a business-like manner, another may be equally good but*

require coaxing into the sort of shot the photographer envisages. Once a model has worked with a photographer for long enough for a rapport to be established she will obviously feel more at ease – and this should come through in the pictures.

The three pictures below were shot with the aid of soft-focus attachments while the others are perfectly straightforward. Note, however, the careful attention that has been paid to colour balance and harmony, and how even the most casual-looking shots show a great deal of care and attention to detail. (Picture above: Hasselblad. All other shots were taken on Mamiya RB67 equipment)

Within reason, a model can look however the photographer wishes. The choice of setting, the background, the choice of colours and their intensity, the clothes, the pose, the degree of sharpness or softness, the angle of a face–all contribute to the final result. There is also the question of how a photographer 'sees' a particular model. She can be used for very sexy shots by one photographer, while another can see her as demure and innocent and portray her that way.

All the pictures on these pages are 'soft' by the use of different techniques: soft focus filters, backlighting forming a spread of light around the model, backlighting through a translucent, patterned screen, the use of a wide aperture producing out of focus colours in the foreground, and even, almost shadowless lighting combined with pastel colours and delicate make-up. (Picture right: Nikon, all other pictures taken on Hasselblad cameras)

The Models

unknown for models to appear at the studio looking as though they had just got out of bed (which they probably had) and horrify the client – unable to believe that this was the model he had accepted for the job or, indeed, that she could ever be made to look anything like her! His confidence then has to be restored, and it is not until the model appears, fully made-up and seemingly transformed (much to his amazement), that this can be accomplished.

Model agencies also tend to specialise in the types of models they have on their books and the work they accept, for instance, glamour, show models for the catwalk, or models suitable for commercial or advertising work. For their services the agencies usually deduct twenty to twenty-five percent of the models' fees, which seems fair, providing they look after the girls well and organise regular work for them.

Unless a photographic session is firmly arranged and is not liable to change, the model can be booked on a provisional basis. This can then be confirmed or cancelled as near as twenty-four hours before the session is due to take place. If the session is abandoned or changed with less notice to the agency, then a cancellation fee will be charged; quite understandably in view of the fact that such short notice of a cancellation will probably mean that the model will not have any work at all at that time.

A clear indication should also be given, at the time of booking a model, as to what accessories will be required; shoes or boots, evening or day wear, particular colours and styles etc., although if a very specific requirement is called for and the model in question cannot meet it, then it is up to the photographer or client to purchase or hire it. It is not reasonable to expect a girl to have every combination of colour and style in her wardrobe, although she may well have more than may be imagined.

If a model works after her normal hours – 5.30 to 6.00 pm – she will expect one and a half times her normal hourly fee, and at weekends up to twice that amount. This, however, can often be negotiated, as it sometimes is in the case of trips abroad, when a fee may be worked out that provides the client with a price below what the model would usually charge on a weekly basis, but that gives her enough, together with the added incentive of flying off to the sun for a week or two, to keep her happy.

At the end of all commercial sessions, models are required to sign a model release form, on which is entered her fee, time worked, client and the use for which the shots will be required. This legally covers the client and the photographer, providing, of course, that the pictures are, indeed, only used for the purposes stated.

Equipment

There is a vast, almost bewildering array of photographic equipment available today, and virtually all of it can be used, more or less successfully, for most photographic work. We must remember, nevertheless, that we are thinking, in the context of this book, about equipment that is ideally suited to girl photography. It must be emphasised, however, that choice of equipment is a very personal thing; a particular camera may be better suited to an individual for the very simple reason that he or she is left eyed, for instance, or the controls may be just where they feel 'right'. Some people find large cameras cumbersome and difficult to handle, while others like the reassurance of a heavy camera and find a small one fiddly to operate. Versatility is obviously important – the facility to accept interchangeable lenses and accessories – but the main judgement must be subjective; the camera should be an extension of *your* hand and eye, so that operating it is an automatic action and all your attention is directed towards the photographs. A model will not feel very confident if she has to wait while you fiddle around with various items of photographic apparatus with which you are obviously not totally familiar.

There are many cameras that are ideally suited to various types of photography but there is no one camera that can be considered absolutely right for every subject. For our purposes, however, there are really only three types of camera that need to be considered: the 35mm, the 6×6cm and the 6×7cm. Although the cameras are quite different in handling and viewing characteristics, most photographers are quite happy to use both 35mm and rollfilm models, depending on the client's particular requirements; nevertheless there is usually one camera the photographer prefers to use, which he feels suits his style, and which he will use whenever possible, no matter what the situation.

All lenses have their uses in photography but wide-angle lenses do cause problems with apparent distortion, particularly when used close to the subject, as in the shot of Felicity above left.

Soft lighting can be very flattering and can, with the right subject and treatment, create a delicate mood in a picture above right *but it is a technique that requires considerable care.*

Soft focus attachments and filters come in a variety of styles and strengths. Some have concentric ridges, some have raised bumps in the glass, others are engraved to break up the surface of the glass. It is, however, important to remember that a real soft focus effect does not destroy definition but has the effect of spreading the highlights, rather as though a second, weaker and broader image was placed over the first. Remember

that the effects of a soft focus attachment are minimised as the lens aperture is closed.

The simplest ways of achieving soft focus is simply to stretch a piece of nylon stocking or similar over the lens and shoot against the light. Some very beautiful effects can be obtained in this way. There are also soft focus filters in which the central area of the picture remains unaffected; the softening effect being confined to the edges of the subject.

The pictures left, far left, below left *and* right *were all shot using varying methods of softening the image but, however it is done it requires experience in order to accurately predict the results.*

The striking shot bottom,

taken in Portugal, was the result of co-operation by the model, recognition of a picture-making possibility by the photographer, superb timing, a fast shutter speed – and luck!

(All pictures: Hasselblad cameras)

Equipment

Cameras

There is no doubt that the dominant camera is now the single lens reflex, particularly in the field of model photography. This is not to say – with regard to 35mm photography – that it is a 'better' camera than the rangefinder model, but it is certainly more convenient, for the purposes we are considering, in several respects. As its name implies, all viewing is carried out through the actual lens in use and there are no frame marks within which to compose the picture; we see, full frame, exactly what the lens sees and, therefore, exactly what will appear on the film. It allows us to see the effects of out-of-focus areas as they will appear, and we can also see what happens when we place various accessories in front of the lens. Metering systems can be built into the camera which are nowadays very accurate indeed – although it must be mentioned that most professionals still tend to use a separate, hand-held meter. The range of lenses available for these cameras is vast; in the 35mm format they are available from 'fish-eye', with a focal length of about 8mm, to telephoto lenses of 1,000mm and more, with zoom lenses covering varying focal lengths within the range. In addition there are motor drives, power winders and so on. The range of lenses and accessories available for the 6×6 and 6×7 single lens reflexes is not quite so comprehensive as that for the 35mm cameras but, nevertheless, it is considerable, and the same remarks with regard to viewing and focusing apply.

These days you can't really go far wrong if you choose a camera bearing a well-known name. They are all made to a high standard, as indeed they have to be if they are to keep their share of what is a very competitive market. The choice depends on the features you consider most useful and, as has already been mentioned, on how the camera feels in your hands, and this is something only you can know.

Red doors, a model and a swirling skirt were enough to produce the simple shot above *for Kodak 'View' magazine.*

For the picture right *the photographer waited until late evening, when the light was just sufficient to record the sky and sea, posed his models – for the swimwear advertisement he was producing – against the Mini-Mokes, and used flash to 'lift' the colours and provide an unusual and striking shot.*

The lovely shot of Willow facing page, left, was made for Arborite Laminates. It was lit by tungsten lighting and consists of one exposure. A picture of Willow was projected onto the laminate-covered letter and she was required to remain still while the exposure, in perfectly balanced lighting, was made. (All pictures: Hasselblads)

Format – 35mm or 6 × 6cm

Speed, ease of handling, a wide choice of lenses and accessories and the ability to take a 36 exposure roll of film are obvious points in favour of the 35mm SLR. A number of professionals, however, prefer the image size of the 6 × 6 or 6 × 7 format. The transparencies this size of camera provides are easier to see and, perhaps more important, are generally preferred by clients. The 6 × 6cm focusing screen is good for composing pictures but the camera, in its standard form, requires that you look down into the viewing hood rather than holding the camera at eye level, and this is something that takes getting used to. There are prism finders available but these are pretty hefty, and usually very expensive, although they do allow you to view at eye level if this is important to you. Such cameras only give eight or twelve exposures per roll,

but this is offset by the ability to interchange magazine backs so, providing you have two or three of these items, shooting can be almost as fast as with a 35mm. One big plus – particularly for professionals – is that the rollfilm SLR will take a Polaroid back, something that is considered virtually essential by many photographers. Most of the SLRs taking 120 film are very similar in handling characteristics, but there is one exception – the Pentax 6 × 7. This camera has the appearance and feel of a large 35mm camera, but is much heavier and bulkier and there is no Polaroid back available through the manufacturer. It is, however, a first class camera and one that handles in a way that is quite familiar to those photographers who spend most of their time working with 35mm but require the larger negatives or transparencies for particular assignments.

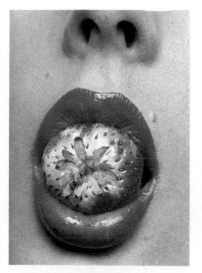

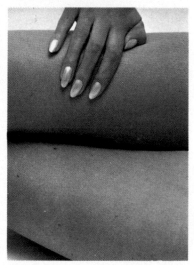

There can surely be no doubt that the shot top *was taken to promote a lipstick, the brand name of which could only be* 'strawberry pink'.

Equally obviously, nail varnish was the subject of the photograph above, *a simple and direct message.*
(Both pictures taken on Nikon cameras)

Equipment

Lenses

For many years photographers – including fashion and model photographers – used cameras with fixed lenses; in particular the ubiquitous Rolleiflex twin lens reflex. This meant that they became totally familiar with the field of view of their one lens and they had to move away from, or nearer to, the subject if they wanted a close-up or a distant view. Nowadays there are lenses available for practically every situation, but there is, perhaps, too much of a tendency to change lenses to try to improve a picture when what is really needed is either a change of viewpoint or a rearrangement of the subject. It would be ridiculous to suggest that interchangeable lenses are not useful, on the contrary, they are invaluable, but to paraphrase the carpenter's old adage that 'it is better to measure twice and cut once' – then it might be worth considering that 'it is better to think twice and change lenses once'.

For most general photography the standard lens – 50mm on a 35mm camera, and 80mm on 6×6 – copes admirably. Rather than go in too close and cause distortions, however, a longer lens is more suitable for head and shoulder shots, while to make a girl appear taller, slimmer, or have longer legs a moderate wide-angle lens is useful. Outdoors, a very long telephoto lens can be effective in throwing everything but the main part of the subject out of focus, and it also gives a flattening, foreshortened look, besides softening the face and body.

There are no real rules as to which lens is 'right' for a subject. Everything must depend on the effect you, as the photographer, want to achieve. By all means experiment, using extreme wide-angle lenses, zooming during exposure and so on, but try not to make a poor picture into a good one by the use of gimmickry – it seldom works.

Meters

There are four basic types of exposure meter: reflected light measuring, incident light measuring, spot measuring (although this is, strictly speaking, a narrow-angle reflected light meter), and the flash meter (again, this is really an incident light meter, but useful only for measuring flash exposures).

Reflected light measuring meters read the intensity of light reflected from a subject. They work at their most effective when they are used close to the subject so that they are not influenced by light reflected from areas other than from the subject. Care should be taken, when using such a meter, that you, or the meter, do not block light which would otherwise fall on the subject, as this will lead to an incorrect reading. Reflected light meters were for many years the standard, hand-held light measuring instrument and there is no doubt that they can provide an excellent guide to exposures.

The incident light meter measures the light actually falling on the subject rather than that reflected from it. It is normally equipped with a white plastic dome. This dome gathers light and should be directed from the subject position towards the camera. In practice, the dome can point towards the camera from any position between camera and subject providing the light falling on the dome is of the same intensity and from the same direction as that falling on the subject. In other words, if the subject is standing in the shade twenty yards away, then the meter must also be held in the shade, even if only in the shade provided by the photographer's body.

Spot meters are now becoming very popular as new models come on the market. They work in much the same way as a camera insofar as the subject is viewed through a viewfinder and lens. In the viewfinder a small circle is marked which denotes the actual light measuring area – usually about 1° – and this is

centred on the chosen area of the subject to be measured. On pressing a trigger, a needle then indicates the exposure required for that small area only. Readings can thus be taken of skin tones, in shadow and in full lighting, and these readings can be taken from some distance away with remarkable accuracy.

A flash meter works in an almost identical way to the incident light meter in that it measures the light falling on the subject, but it is specially made and calibrated for electronic flash. The meter is connected into the flash circuit and pointed at the camera position from the subject. Pressing a button on the meter itself then fires the flash and the meter indicates the exposure required.

Exposure meters, of whatever type, whether built into the camera or hand-held, are not a magic recipe for unfailingly accurate exposures. Like any other piece of equipment, they can be fooled, and it is up to the operator to understand the meter he is working with and to know how to interpret the information it gives him, so as to arrive at the final result – the picture – that he wants.

Tripods

Some photographers can hand-hold cameras at quite low shutter speeds – or they like to think they can! If, however, you compare photographs taken at the same shutter speed but with the camera hand-held for one shot and placed on a sturdy tripod for the next, then the difference in quality will usually be readily apparent. Although some cameras are easier for some people to hand-hold steadily than are others, there is still no doubt that the single biggest cause of unsharp pictures is camera shake. A number of photographers try to do without tripods whenever they can because they are, to be honest, heavy and cumbersome things to carry around. The answer is, however, not a tripod that is light and compact, and that will slip into the gadget bag easily. Such a tripod is unlikely to be of any use and you would be better off with a good, solid, table-top tripod that can be braced against a wall or some other stationary object.

Tripods come in all sizes and it is important to choose one that is substantial enough to support your camera. If you are in doubt then it is best to seek advice from your dealer.

Studio tripods or camera stands are usually very heavy, substantial items. It is not uncommon to see a 35mm or 6×6cm camera mounted on a huge, single-column camera stand that is easily capable of supporting a 5×4 or even a 10×8 camera. Such stands normally have wheels fitted to them so that they can be moved around the studio easily, but even these wheels can be retracted to provide an even more solid support. A studio stand, or tripod, leaves the photographer free to dash around the studio, but it does not, of course, allow the freedom and mobility of a hand-held camera. As with most things, there are times when one has to be sacrificed for the other.

***Wide-angle lenses were used** for three of the pictures on these pages, not, primarily, to include a wider picture angle but to take advantage of the depth of field such lenses permit. In each case the photographers wanted to feature the foreground – the table, the beautifully-shaped shells, the girl on the sun-lounger – but at the same time render the background reasonably sharp. This can be done fairly easily with a camera equipped with swings, but failing that, a wide-angle lens stopped down as far as possible, using the inevitable distortion as part of the design, is the best solution.*

A cross-star attachment caught the highlights and produced the interesting pattern in the shot of Jenny far left. (Picture top: Bronica, left: Nikon, facing page: Hasselblads)

Equipment

Filters

Polarising Quite apart from its scientific applications, a polarising filter is useful for reducing, or removing altogether, reflections from most surfaces – except metal. The filter has a factor of about 1·5 – which means the exposure must be increased by this amount – and it has an interesting effect on skin, removing highlights and shine. It also tends to enrich colours and make skin appear browner and blue skies deeper in tone. Water – sea or pool – with reflections removed obviously appears far clearer.

Skylight (or 1A) This filter reduces the ultra-violet light that is always present in daylight. Many photographers leave such a filter on their lenses all the time as, in addition to removing excess blue and making the skin appear warmer and more pleasing to the eye, it protects the lens from the detrimental effects of sand, salt, water and all the other bits of debris that are so often blown around in the wind when shooting outdoors.

Star filters There are many variations of this filter, which produces a star of light from highlights, streetlamps, or other light sources. They can be useful, but the effect can easily become tiresome and appear gimmicky.

Diffusers Sometimes called softars, or soft focus filters, they come in various strengths and have the effect of spreading highlights into the rest of the subject. With the best of these attachments the picture still appears sharp but has a pleasing softness about it that can look very flattering.

Graduated filters As their name implies, these filters are graduated from top to bottom, from clear to a deep colour. They come in many different colours and can be combined so as to make a sky darker and, at the same time, a sea greener.

Film

There are so many different types and speeds of film, all with different characteristics, that the choice has to be a very personal one. All you can do is to try different makes and see which one works best for you. There is a lot to be said, however, for sticking to one film, once you have made a choice, until you know exactly how that film will behave in all the situations you are likely to encounter, rather than keep chopping and changing film types and never understanding any of them.

Professionals usually buy film in large batches, which can then be stored in a freezer, and they test one or two rolls to check for any variations in speed and colour. Different batches of the same make of film can fluctuate and adjustments may have to be made with regard to film speed settings and filtration.

Once film has been exposed the processing laboratory will normally carry out a 'clip test' which involves cutting a short length from a film and processing it to make sure that everything is in order before processing the whole result of a session.

An interesting effect can be achieved by exposing daylight film to artificial light, which results in warm, mellow, yellow, orange and brown shots, or artificial light film can be exposed in daylight, which produces an overall blue cast in the transparencies.

Filters are useful for a variety of purposes. The UV absorbing filter serves, in addition to its prime function of reducing the excess blue that is present in light at high altitudes, at midday, and by the sea, to protect the lens and can be left almost permanently in place.

Colour-correcting filters are useful for modifying the colour temperature of light to match more closely that of the film being used – to expose daylight film in artificial light, or vice-versa, for instance. A colour shot can be made almost to resemble a toned print right

and facing page, top left and top centre. *Filters are available, or can easily be made, which have a clear centre left, and filters designed for black and white photography can be particularly effective in against-the-light colour shots facing page, top. A filter consisting of three different coloured segments was used for the picture below but, with care, three different coloured gels could have been combined and held in front of the lens just as effectively. (Picture left: Nikon. All other pictures: Hasselblads)*

Lighting

Simplest is best. This is a reasonable maxim to follow when lighting girls for photography. If you keep it simple you really can't go far wrong, but, if you surround a girl with lights, as many people do, then she will probably end up with cross-shadows, patchy looking skin and you will have an untidy shot that will certainly not please you, the model, or, most important, the client.

To understand lighting requires only that you look. Position a light, switch it on, and see what it does to the subject as you move it. Add another light, or a reflector, and watch, carefully, the difference it makes. Keep doing this, paying attention only to the subject and how light changes it, until you understand the meaning of 'painting with light'. You must understand fully what the light is actually doing, the effect it is having on the face, figure or garment. The type of light you use is also important. A hard light can be used if the subject is as near perfect as possible, but for anyone less than perfect – and this means the majority – then you should use soft lighting, either by bouncing the light off a white card, umbrella or cine screen, or by covering the light with some sort of diffusing material such as tracing paper or spun glass.

Although the term 'painting with light' can properly be applied to all photography, it becomes rather more pertinent when light itself, rather than lighting, is used to create part of the picture, as in the examples shown on these pages.

The technique is not difficult, requiring only a model, a dark background, one, two or more handlamps or torches, preferably someone to assist you – and as many ideas as you can think up.

As models become more experienced they obviously learn more about photographic methods, not necessarily from the point of view of the photographer, but rather what is expected of them as the subject of the picture. They learn when to change poses and expressions, and will often do so each time

they hear the shutter fire or see the lights flash – unless, of course, they are specifically asked to keep perfectly still.

There are minor variations in the way photographs such as these can be taken but the basic method works as follows: the model is placed in position against a dark background, posed as required, and asked to remain still. The lights are switched off and a torch or handlamp (or two or more taped together) is then held by the photographer or assistant, behind the model and directed at the camera, the shutter of which is now opened. The lamp is now switched on and moved at the right speed and in the required pattern to form

the image that is wanted. At the end of the 'pattern' the torch is switched off, the person holding it gets out of the way, and the electronic flash is fired to record the image of the model. The lamp can, of course, be switched on and off where desired to create blobs of light instead of streaks, and various coloured filters can be placed over the lamp or lamps. (All pictures taken with Hasselblad cameras)

Lighting

The series of photographs shown here illustrate the different effects that can be obtained by changing the light source slightly, or merely by adding a white card or mirror.

Heads
1. 1 light
2. 1 light plus fill
3. 1 light plus fill and hair light
4. 1 soft light
5. 1 soft light plus white card under chin
6. 1 soft light plus mirror under chin
7. Direct hand flash

The white card bounces some of the light back, making for a softer effect and filling in the shadow areas under the chin and in and around the eyes. The mirror has a similar but stronger effect, giving the eyes an added lift by producing a second highlight – the first being from the light source – and by making the lips appear very glossy, moist and sensuous.

Small, hand flash units would appear to be basically the province of the amateur snapshooter, but they can, in fact, be very successful in professional use if they are properly understood. The hand flash unit may be used to its best advantage by placing it directly above the camera lens, as this position gives an almost shadowless result which can be most flattering.

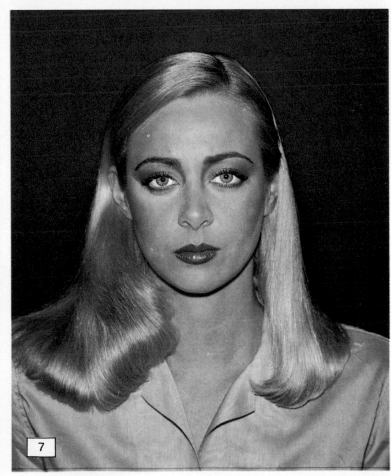

Lighting

The ring flash was originally designed for use in medical photography, where shadowless lighting was required and there was insufficient space to allow lights to be set up near the subject. Such units have now been adopted by many professionals for use in girl photography as they give a soft result with, sometimes, an almost unreal look. Their main drawback is that, being designed primarily for close-up work, ring flash units are not very powerful and they do not have the capacity to recharge quickly, as do the big studio units.

The studio of today is almost invariably equipped with electronic flash, as opposed to the hot, electricity-consuming tungsten lighting of yesterday – which was, indeed, so hot and bright that the subject would often have to screw her eyes up against the glare.

Electronic flash these days comes in many different forms. There is the simple, point light source that can be fitted with various different types of reflectors and snoots, a 3ft × 2ft light

For both the shots on this page a very ordinary background was used. For the picture left a gloss-painted wall was employed which bounced highlights back, directly toward the position of the main flash. For the shot of Nina below, Peter angled the flash head lower, to place the reflection where he wanted it, and dressed his model in a contrasting, green outfit.

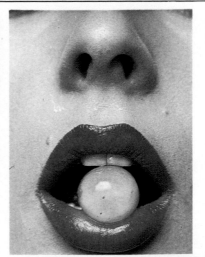

A low-powered flash technique was used for the shot of Nina, top left, *which allowed Peter to use a wide aperture and move in close, throwing the background out of focus and creating its interesting pattern of highlights.*

The grape idea left *was shot simply as an idea to present to a cosmetics manufacturer for a possible lipstick advert.*

Strong primary colours lit by direct flash were used for the picture of Karen left. *This, too, was shot as an idea, with no particular client in mind. Time spent on such ideas is seldom wasted, however, as they often suggest just the kind of shot a client may not think of until* he sees something on film. *The striking study* above *was produced by the use of strong, directional lighting with coloured gels over the flash heads; the predominant colour being green, with an orange light at the left. (Top picture: Nikon, all others: Hasselblads)*

Lighting

The outlandish make-up and outfit below were selected to complement the equally unusual hairstyle which was the real reason for the session. Both this shot, of Joley, and the one facing page top right, of Wilma, were produced for a Japanese hairdresser, to show his various styles. When shooting such commissions it is obviously of the utmost importance for the photographer to know exactly the total look the artist envisages.

The session below was set up for Littlewoods, the mail order catalogue company, and the outfit the girl is modelling is meant to echo the designer's interpretation of a 'forties' look. To emphasise this feeling, the male model was dressed as a U.S. serviceman and the set was also chosen to suggest the same period. Such a shot must, of course, concentrate on the clothing being featured and all else must be secondary to it.

Constant experimentation with ideas and techniques is the photographer's lifeblood. The striking shots of Viva, facing page, top left, and Nina bottom right were both taken as experiments, but the ability to produce them inevitably led to commissions for other work in these and similar styles.

The girl on the motorcycle right was photographed for a motorbike advertisement; the object being, firstly, to attract attention to the girl, and thence to the machine. While this may be fairly obvious, the reason for the shot of Viva facing page, bottom left may not be so clear. It was, in fact, taken for the manufacturer of the webbing she wears round her waist and wrists. (All pictures taken on Hasselblads)

Lighting

An artist's eye and a high degree of technical skill were required to produce the optical illusion below. There is, in fact, very little space behind the model. The converging lines were drawn, to follow the lines in the foreground, when viewed from the camera position, and the two different sized balls, and the sky, were added to increase the illusion of distance.

The head shot of Joanne top right *was taken for a cosmetics company, and that* centre right *for a hair colouring brochure.*

The evocative study above right *was first conceived as a high key, white subject. Backlighting produced the gentle, luminous quality of the drapery and sufficient light was reflected back into the model to preserve the delicacy of the mood without overpowering the backlighting. For some of the shots a pale magenta filter was used, which produced this delicate effect. Note that the photographer posed his model in such a way that she was actually using her hands, and the whole situation just becomes believable, as does the picture right. In this, the hands are again put to use, and the accessories create the idea that this is a study of a ballet dancer. (All pictures: Hasselblad cameras)*

Hands can prove a problem, *as already mentioned. They can be used, however, as part of the picture design below. This shot had to be taken directly above the model to allow her hair to be arranged in this way.*

Soft focus should not be confused with out of focus. Soft focus allows the highlights to spread, without destroying sharpness. The picture right is normal, and that far right is soft focus. Note that the catchlights in the eyes in both shots are equally sharp. (All pictures: Hasselblads)

Lighting

box – known as a 'fish fryer' – and a 5ft × 3ft light box – called a 'swimming pool' – both of which provide a lovely, soft, even light, producing large highlights in the eyes etc. Then there are soft lights which, as well as projecting a tiny point of light, can also project any desired shape of mask, such as stars, diamonds, squares, crescents and so on. The quality of light provided by electronic flash, properly handled, is said to be the closest to that of daylight which, of course, is considered to have a quality all its own.

When photographing a girl on a plain paper background in the studio, it is important to light the background as well as the subject. Failing to do this will result in light fall off, the background will go too dark, and shadows will be thrown on it from the subject. One way of lighting the background is to place a light on each side – ideally fitted with diffusers to help spread the light evenly – but making sure that the lights are directed only at the background and are not allowed to spill either onto the subject or into the camera lens. An alternative method is to place one, two or more spot lights, taking care in their positioning and carefully observing the effect that each additional light has on both the subject and background.

To take exposure readings with electronic flash, a flash meter

is normally used. This is an exposure meter made for measuring the light intensity of flash and cannot be used for any other type of exposure measurement. The meter is either plugged into the flash unit, which means that it is coupled into the circuit, and the flash can be fired by a control on the meter itself, or it may be used by firing the flash independently, without the use of a lead. Such meters are always of the incident light measuring type, which means that they measure the light falling on the subject rather than that reflected from it. The meter is, therefore, held at the subject position with the light gathering dome pointed directly at the camera. A reading can then be taken indicating the exposure that should be used for the main subject. Next, a reading should be taken from the background position, again with the dome directed at the camera, and this will indicate whether or not the lighting level is the same for subject and background. If the background is to be of a similar density to that of the main subject, then the readings should be equal. It may be that it is considered desirable that the intensity of light on the background should be a little stronger than that on the subject. This has the effect of cleaning up the background slightly. This is, of course, all a matter of personal preference and, although there are rules, or guidelines, for lighting, these may always be broken and, when they are, the best pictures sometimes result.

Carefully controlled studio *lighting is evident in all the subjects on these pages, which were shot in the studios of Beverley Goodway. The electronic flash used is equipped – as are most studio units these days – with modelling lights. These are ordinary light bulbs fitted in the same position as the flash tubes, allowing an assessment to be made of the exact effect the flash will have. Electronic flash is very powerful and needs 'taming' for soft, feminine subjects. This can be done by reflecting the light, using umbrellas or white polystyrene 'flats', both of which soften the light. By using several*

flash heads it is possible to achieve a result similar to that produced by daylight coming through a window. A light on a boom above the model's head can be used to cause a 'halo' of backlighting which works very well with less than formal hairstyles.

Before rushing out and spending a great deal of money on elaborate flash outfits, it is as well to learn to appreciate and understand light. Watch how light coming through a window behaves; how strong sunlight produces a quite different effect from soft, overcast light. See what happens when you position something light – a newspaper perhaps – in the path of the sunlight, to reflect it back

into the shadows. **Learn to observe light at all times**; it is only too easy to be disappointed by the results of a session – for which you have used special equipment – simply because the feeling you had for what you wanted only existed in your mind, and the camera could only record what was in front of it. Good lighting requires patience, experimentation, but still, most of all, observation. In this set of pictures all the backgrounds and outfits have been chosen with great care to produce shots that are in regular demand for magazines, calendars and advertising.

(All pictures: Mamiya RB67 cameras)

Location Photography

Once the details of a trip, such as the choice of models, make-up artist, props (if required), type and quantity of film, accessories and so on have been worked out, the next thing that may be considered is whether or not a carnet is required. A carnet is a form of licence that allows the import and export of equipment to and from different countries and obviates the worry of equipment perhaps being impounded by customs authorities – sometimes for days or even weeks. In exchange for the issuing of a carnet, money must be lodged with the appropriate government department sufficient to meet the cost of the equipment should it not be returned to the country designated on the carnet as the country of origin. Most countries nowadays accept and comply with the carnet system, but it must be pointed out that it is not completely foolproof. A carnet involves numerous forms which, in

All the pictures on these pages *were taken in the West Indies, on the island of Antigua, for Silhouette swimwear. For such an assignment it must be borne in mind that the prime consideration is to show the clothes – on this occasion swimsuits and beachwear – to their best advantage. Such treatments as soft focus foregrounds below can be used, but sparingly. Obviously, the models must look good, as the reasoning behind such advertising has to be geared to the idea that the clothes will make every woman look stunning. Knowing exactly which clothes will be photographed means that all the accessories can be chosen before the trip and, once on location, the trick is to find the best settings and props to display the models – and clothes – to the client's satisfaction. (All pictures taken on Hasselblad cameras)*

Location Photography

theory at least, all have to be signed at various stages of the journey – both outward and inward – by the customs authorities of each country for which the carnet is valid. It will be seen, therefore, that arriving in a country in the early hours of the morning when there may be no-one on duty responsible for signing the appropriate form could, technically, cause problems. Nevertheless, the carnet system works well enough in practice and is as much as can be done to ensure free passage of equipment and a successful trip.

Another point that is worth considering is whether or not to take out weather insurance, whereby, if the weather turns out to be really bad in the chosen location, and shooting is impossible then, providing a specified amount of rain has fallen, the insurance company will reimburse the client so that the job may be set up again later, when the weather has improved.

Once on location – it may be in a jungle, a desert or in the mountains – it may well prove impossible to have a camera repaired, to buy more Polaroid film, or even to obtain something as simple as another bottle of baby oil. It is essential, therefore, that a sufficient quantity of equipment and supplies is taken at the outset: several camera bodies, a good selection of lenses, so that if one fails there is another of a close enough focal length to take

The choice of model – in this case Jenny Clare – the hairstyle, clothes, accessories and location all seem to come together perfectly in the series of pictures on this page to evoke a feeling of peace and tranquillity. The combination of a very lovely model and an old cottage and garden in the English countryside is an idea that is hard to resist, and it was exactly this atmosphere and feeling that the photographer sought to convey.

All the pictures were shot on the same day – fortunately in ideal weather for the subject – with fairly soft light, and it is quite obvious that Jenny reacted perfectly to the mood the photographer wanted.

The camera chosen for this particular assignment was a Nikon, and the photographer took with him a variety of lenses although he used, primarily, the 35mm and the 50mm. For some shots he used these lenses at open apertures to create out of focus backgrounds, but he also used a soft focus attachment as well as employing the old trick of smearing petroleum jelly around the edge of a piece of plain glass to achieve edge softening in some pictures.

Before shooting, it is essential to know not only the sort of pictures you want to take, but also the feeling you wish to convey. The object of the two pictures top was to suggest a peaceful, timeless quality and the location chosen was the island of Minorca. (Both shots taken on Hasselblad cameras)

In contrast, the shot above is entirely a product of its time and the pose suggests a happy, carefree lifestyle in keeping with the outfit.

Although carefully set up, the picture left suggests an unguarded moment caught by the camera and has a distinct voyeuristic appeal. (Picture above: Nikon. Left: a 35mm camera was used but no details are available)

Location Photography

The locations for the pictures on these pages range from Europe to the Mediterranean and beyond, to as far away as the West Indies. Photographers do not choose to go to faraway places – and, indeed, clients do not sanction the high costs involved – just for the pleasure of seeing new places. Planning overseas trips can be costly, time-consuming and the trip itself can be fraught with all kinds of problems. Weather obviously plays an important part in deciding to go to a sunny climate although good weather is by no means as reliable as might be imagined, wherever you go. Nevertheless, sunshine and quality of light can at least be counted on for most of the time if the right season is chosen. What an overseas location does give us is a new landscape, new architecture, a different way of life – and different picture-making possibilities waiting to be exploited.

Mediterranean sunlight has a beautiful, luminous quality and it was this light, plus the typical architecture, and its colour, to be found in the area, that the photographer employed so successfully in the picture right, *in which the model, Nina, is wearing an improvised outfit that harmonises ideally with the pale blue of the doorway. In the same way, the angular pose adopted by Nina* above, far right *echoes the shapes on the wall and window, while the word 'graffiti' ties in with the writing above her. The darkly exotic look of Carol* above right *has been used to good effect in the banana plantation setting and the model's clothes, the way they are worn, and her attitude equally harmonise with the setting of the shot* below right. *The harshening effect of strong sunlight has been avoided* below, far right *by placing the girl in the shade while allowing some sunlight to splash onto her body, her hair, and the harvested crop she is carrying. (All pictures taken with Hasselblad equipment)*

Location Photography

over, and, of course, a plentiful supply of film. There is nothing more annoying than finding, at the end of a session, that there is one more shot that could be done – not necessarily one that has already been planned – and there is not enough film to cover it.

For location work, in addition to the usual exposure meter, a spot meter is a very useful piece of equipment to have on hand so that accurate reading can be taken of skin tones when the model is in the sea, or up a tree, without the photographer having to join her! (Although accurate exposure readings are preferable in every case, it is worth mentioning, however, that it is fairly safe to expose 64 ASA film at the equivalent of 1/125 at f8 providing the girl is in direct sunlight on a clear, sunny day).

If anything, the aim should be to underexpose slightly, rather than overexpose, transparency film, as this has the effect of enriching the colours. A polarising filter is useful (remembering to

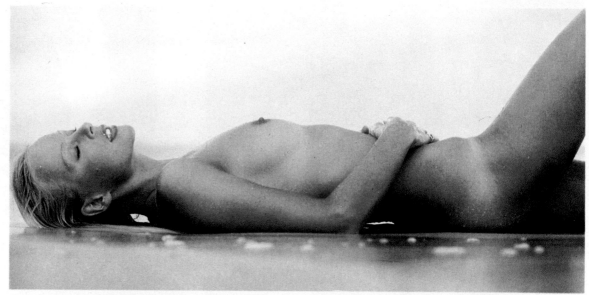

Sunshine is not always as reliable as might be expected, even in the West Indies, where the shots above and centre right were taken. During this particular trip there were days when the clouds were very thick. It was this heavy sky that prompted the shot of Annie lying flat on the sand to create this horizontal composition.

In marked contrast is the picture right, in which the model is lying down primarily to avoid the heavy shadows that would be so apparent due to the position of the sun almost overhead.

The colour-intensifying properties of a polarising filter are shown to advantage top right, while the model top left used the dress she was wearing to create interest in what would have been a relatively static composition. (All pictures taken using Hasselblad equipment)

Strong, bright sunlight invariably causes problems of contrast. The effect can be lessened by placing the model where light can be reflected back into the shadows above, or attention can be drawn away from the problem by the use of strong colours and eye-catching props in other parts of the picture far left.

One obvious way of avoiding heavy shadows is to use the shade of, for instance, an umbrella left. A reflector was also used to bounce light back into the subject. Note the soft, golden light, the use of yellow accessories, and the oil used to impart a sheen to the model's skin.

Location Photography

All three subjects on this page feature diagonals as strong elements of their composition. For the shot of Nina *right* a wide-angle lens was used to emphasise the convergence of the steps and the hand rails *(even though this, inevitably, meant some distortion of her legs, minimised to a certain extent by their careful positioning), and in the picture below right she was posed in such a way that the lines of her body followed the main diagonal except for the opposing effect on her right leg. The lines of the cart below were, however, already balanced by the shape of the wheel and the cart was therefore used simply as a background, serving also to enhance the rustic feeling of the shot.*
(All pictures taken using Hasselblad equipment)

When Peter Barry saw the *picture-making possibilities of this graffiti and poster-covered wall in London right, he knew that, in order to make the shot he had in mind work, he would want to keep to the colour scheme already present. He could simply have posed his model, Jenny, elegantly dressed, and relied on the incongruity that would have resulted for the picture's impact, but he particularly wanted to show a reason for her being there.*

The outfit that was chosen was casual and colourful and, in contrast to the wall, outstandingly clean and fresh, its brightness together with Jenny's hair and carefully-applied make-up completing the contrast. The paint and brush were enough to supply the reason for her being there and electronic flash was used to expose the film in a Hasselblad camera.

Location Photography

allow for a filter factor of approximately 1½ stops) to make the sky appear bluer, the sea more transparent and richer in colour, and the girl browner. Baby oil on the girl's skin is essential in producing a glistening, sensuous look but care must be taken to ensure that sand does not stick to her, perhaps spoiling the shot – although it must be said that it can look great for the occasional picture. The oil will have the effect of 'cooking' the model if she is in strong sunlight, unless she is already very brown. A water spray creates a lovely wet look, with sparkling droplets of water – and also serves to cool the model.

A good supply of medicines and protective creams to offset the effects of insect bites, and the sun, should be taken along on a trip as, out of every three or four girls who all insist that they do not burn in the sun, there is always one who will burn badly and be unable to work for several days. If a girl looks likely to burn she must be made to sun herself in easy stages no matter how adamant she is about not burning. It seems that models just do not like admitting that they burn. Every precaution should also be taken to try to ensure that the girls do not get bitten or stung by insects as this can mean red bumps and swellings, once again making it impossible for them to work.

When working on location in bright sunlight it is advisable to shoot either early or late in the day, avoiding shooting at midday. The harsh light and high sun position at midday causes ugly shadows on the girl's face and body unless she can be shielded from it in some way. When the sun is lower, and if the girl is facing

into it, this causes problems with watering, half-closed eyes and in this situation it is advisable to get her to look down or away from the sun, or to close her eyes, until the moment of exposure. If, however, you shoot her against the sun, not only do you not have this problem but you also have a very soft, flattering light with a halo around the girl. In this case it is advisable to use a reflector to bounce some of the light back into her face, which helps to reduce the contrast between shadow areas and highlights. The reflector can be just a white card, a newspaper, a piece of white material or something similar. Silver, gold or white plastic reflectors are available which fold up very small indeed, but these are usually so flimsy that in even a slight breeze there are problems in keeping them in place. It should also be mentioned that the silver or gold reflectors, although useful for providing a colder or warmer colour balance, are also highly reflective and do tend to cause glare, which again affects the model's eyes so, on balance, the

A hotel balcony in Portugal was the setting for the picture far left. It provided good, open shade, and soft, even light which is very flattering. The model, Jaleh, had exactly the right colouring to harmonise with the walls and floor of the balcony, and the bougainvillaea suggested the appropriate colour for her dress. The pose was simple and reflective; the inclination of the head gave just the right modelling to Jaleh's features and, very important, enough space was left at the right of the frame to give her an area to 'look into'.

Another centrally-placed figure in a composition is shown top left, *and this also works well for much the same reason as the picture of Jaleh: the head is turned away from the direction in which the body is facing and the eye is consequently held by the figure. All the clothes required, together with such items as matching parasols, hats,*

jewellery and all the other accessories have to be chosen well before a location assignment starts, and they are one of the reasons why models and photographers always seem to travel with an enormous number of suitcases.

Photographing the nude indoors, in privacy, presents no real problems other than those of a technical nature, as in the beautifully backlit shot of Stephanie left. Outdoors, however, the story is quite different and unless a totally secluded location is chosen, something that is becoming increasingly difficult to find, then timing is all-important, as is pre-planning so that the model is nude for the briefest time possible, which was how the shot of Nina Carter bottom left was accomplished. It was taken not, as might be thought, in the American Midwest, but outside a small hotel in Tunisia, decorated to resemble a Western Saloon. Obviously, in such a situation the last thing wanted is a crowd of onlookers and there is, additionally, the problem of causing offence, or even being accused of breaking the law. The model, therefore, would normally wear a light coat or some other covering until the last possible moment when, with everything set up, she would hand it to an assistant for the few moments while the shot, or shots, were taken. (All pictures these pages: Hasselblad equipment)

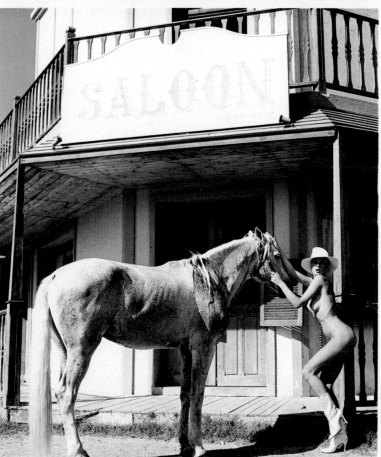

Location Photography

There are many ways in which an ordinary subject can be turned into a visually exciting or 'different' one. For the startling shot *left* the photographer shot straight down at the model who was lying on an airbed in a swimming pool, and had an assistant splash water over her. He used a 35mm camera and the fastest shutter speed possible – even to the point of slight underexposure – to render at least some of the water droplets sharp, and thus provide the impact he wanted in the picture.

A wide-angle lens – 50mm – was used to exaggerate perspective in the shot of Patsy on the balcony *top left, part of* the picture being softened by the use of petroleum jelly on a piece of glass held in front of the lens.

In the strong mid-day sun, Peter Barry posed his model in the shade of a palm tree *top right, using the cast shadows of* the leaves as part of the design of his picture.

Strong backlighting was employed for both the straightforward shot of Stephanie *above* and that of Tina *left,* taken in Grenada, in the West Indies. For this shot Peter left Tina's body in shadow but used a hand mirror to reflect sunlight back into her face.

(All pictures on this page: Hasselblad cameras)

Location Photography

softer effect of the white reflector is probably preferable.

A big advantage of working on location is that there are obviously no area restrictions or limitations as there are in the studio. There are no electronic flash power packs, lighting stands or sync leads, mains leads and so on to make the photographer feel that he is involved in some sort of obstacle course. On the other hand, outdoor shooting presents its own problems, not least of which are waiting for clouds to pass, the wind to die down and stop blowing the model's hair all over her face, and waiting for people to move out of shot. There is the additional problem of looking after equipment outdoors; not just keeping an eye on it, but trying to ensure that sand and salt water are kept out of the mechanism.

Obviously, in high-risk locations such as beaches and deserts, equipment should be thoroughly cleaned after each day's work and it is also advisable to keep a skylight filter over the lens at all times, both to filter out the excess blue and to protect the vulnerable lens from the elements.

When shooting outdoors the actual choice of location is very much a personal thing, but it should be remembered that the background should enhance and complement the girl and must certainly not compete with her. It is also useful to look for a foreground through which to shoot, as well as objects for the girl to sit on, or things with which she can become involved, thus adding credence to the shots.

and can usually be hired quite reasonably in such places as the Bahamas, the Mediterranean, the West Indies etc. There is, however, restricted space, and therefore camera angles, on a boat. Because of this, a wide-angle lens is obviously useful, and the distortion this produces can be put to good effect in suggesting distance, as in the

shot *facing page, top left*. One of the boat's most useful functions is that it provides the possibility of using, when near to land, ever-changing backgrounds *facing page, bottom left*.

Geometric shapes accentuated by a wide-angle lens provided the ideal setting for the shot of Nina, taken in Tunisia *facing page, top right*.

A girl's body can be used to create an interesting shape *above* to contrast with a regular, ordered background, but a photographer should always be on the lookout for shapes and patterns he can combine with the model, as in the picture *left* where a window was used as a somewhat precarious perch, and Nina adopted a stance that opposed the rectangular feeling of the window and wall.

The window *facing page, bottom right* was used as an integral part of the composition; the model's outfit being chosen to blend with rather than contrast her surroundings.
(*All pictures: Hasselblads*)

Studio Photography

Studios are usually as large as is practicable – or available – and painted white or black – more often black. White walls obviously reflect light, so if black is used then the photographer has complete control over the lighting, including any that may be reflected onto the subject. He can easily add reflecting surfaces if he so wishes, but it is by no means so easy to blank out white areas if he does not want them.

A good selection of rolls of coloured background paper – as well as fittings from which to hang them – is essential.

Background paper usually comes in widths of approximately nine to twelve feet, and in a range of about thirty colours. One of the advantages of such papers is that they can be lit so as to provide an even tone behind the model without any distracting lines – for instance, where the wall and floor meet – running across her.

For a comprehensively-equipped studio, electronic flash equipment of between 5,000 and 30,000 joules will be required, together with various types of flash heads; fish fryers, spotlights, background strip lighting, ring lights and all-purpose heads.

Carefully controlled and balanced lighting are the hallmarks of good studio photography. In the set of pictures on these pages Beverley Goodway displays his mastery of studio technique in a stunning set of pictures, all featuring Sian Adey-Jones.

Backgrounds have been chosen to complement, contrast or harmonise with both the model and the mood of each shot and there are also

obvious or subtle changes in the lighting. Sian's hairstyle has also been changed, again to match the mood. The severity of the shot top, far right would have been impaired had a similar hairstyle to that of the other shots been used.

A fan, and backlighting, were combined to produce the beautiful effect left. (All pictures taken using Mamiya RB67 equipment)

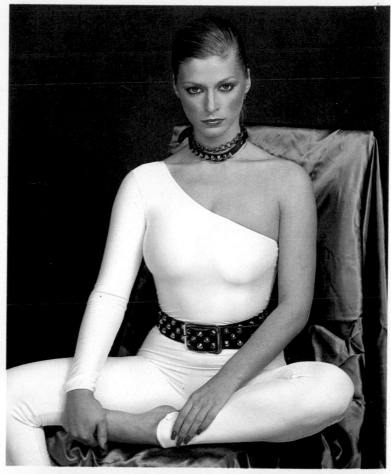

Studio Photography

A sturdy tripod, or a single-column camera stand, is vital to the studio layout, and another useful item is a professional wind machine capable of producing really strong wind effects, although a desk fan is often sufficient to blow a girl's hair or a flimsy garment. On this subject, it is wise to take care with wind machines; if they are used for too long they tend to tire the model's eyes, making them sore, and maybe, red. It is therefore advisable to let her rest after every one or two rolls of film.

Music is often considered important, both to relax everyone in the studio, and to help to create an atmosphere – be it soft, dreamy and romantic, or earthy and sexy. For this purpose the latest sounds are usually the most suitable as everyone will know them well and they won't prove too distracting.

A collection of sheets of white, coloured and black cards are very useful accessories for reflecting light back into a subject, shielding light from the camera lens, or even as a background or foreground in a shot. Equally useful is a selection of coloured gels, both for colouring the light, and for shooting through, so as to create a band of colour around the subject, and various sized mirrors may be used to reflect strong, bright light onto the subject, to provide catchlights in the eyes or highlights on the lips.

A full-length mirror, on wheels, placed near the camera helps the model to see what the camera is seeing, so that she can check her position, hair and make-up, but it is always best to check with the girl whether she wants the mirror or not as some girls find it very disturbing to see themselves and would rather do without it.

A dressing room should, ideally, be connected to the studio and it should be equipped with a hair dryer, heated hair rollers, a selection of make-up, a robe for the model to wear while she is getting ready – particularly important in avoiding marks on light coloured underwear – towels, tissues and, most important of all, a mirror with good, bright lighting, at which she can apply her make-up. Other items might include bottles of baby oil, useful for imparting a nice, healthy shine; making the girl look hot and 'tropical'; bringing out the colour of her skin and adding a look of 'roundness' to her body, and a water spray such as the small, hand-held ones used by gardeners, to cover the model's body with tiny water-droplets, and, of course, a supply of ice cubes which the girl can use to firm her nipples in figure shots.

A rail of varied types of outer and underwear is useful to have as a standby for those occasions when the model arrives with an insufficient supply of clothes, or accessories that do not match a particular outfit, as is a selection of stockings, shoes, hats, jewellery, body stockings or any other small items that may seem worthless at most times but are just what is required for the one shot that matters.

Gas cylinders might not be *thought of as ideal props to use for a nude shot, but a little imagination was all that was necessary for Peter Barry to see the possibilities of having Nina wear red stockings and a red scarf to match the red cylinders and produce the shot far left. Whether the red stockings suggested the use of the red cylinders, or vice-versa, is not, however, known!*

A studio large enough to take a vehicle – in this case a New

York cab top, *specially imported for publicity purposes – is useful, but costly to run unless it is regularly used for large sets.*

On the other hand, a surprisingly small studio can be utilised for set-ups such as the beautifully arranged and lit subject left *shot for a wedding dress maker. (All pictures: Hasselblads)*

Studio Photography

A long wig, a model, Tina, recently returned from location abroad and therefore suntanned, some canvas and a brown background with a light directed onto it behind the model, were the only ingredients used for the picture right.

Because of its uncomprising style – its starkness – with no props, it is either a shot that works for the viewer or not.

The shot below, taken by the same photographer, Peter Barry, provides a complete contrast. In this, the hairstyle, make-up, drapery and jewellery have all been chosen to project a mood; an air of sophisticated elegance.

Confetti dropped in front of Viva's face at the moment of exposure was the method used to add splashes of colour to the shot above.
(All pictures: Hasselblads)

The make-up artist and the hair stylist – both of whom are usually creative artists in their own right – created the looks on this page, for Peter Barry to photograph.

The camera has a very critical eye. Unlike our own, which can be fooled very easily, it records, objectively, whatever we place in front of it. As photographers we therefore have to observe all details with the same critically objective eye; the fact that we may find the model charming, amusing or interesting should have nothing to do with the way we view her. We have to examine – particularly in make-up shots like those on this page – every detail of the make-up; whether it appears symmetrical if it should; whether the lighting shows the make-up as we want to see it; how the hair looks, and whether it helps to create the completeness we are aiming for; where the catchlights appear in the eyes, and so on. Only when we are competely satisfied should the shutter be fired.
(All pictures: Hasselblads)

Problems

Most people would admit that, in their particular line of work, problems can arise, and this is so very true of photography in general and model photography in particular; sometimes to the point that the problems never seem to end!

The first, and most irritating of these, is equipment that goes wrong – cameras that jam, or fall apart, flash equipment that overheats or proves unreliable, flash meters that refuse to function, and so on. No matter how good or expensive the equipment, it seems that if it is going to let you down, it will do so at the worst time possible. To try to at least cut down on the possibilities of this happening, it is wise to have hard-working equipment checked over at least once every six months.

Film can be a problem, too. It can sometimes vary from its rated speed, and sometimes you can find a batch of film that has a marked colour shift; so much so that the manufacturer recommends the use of a colour correcting filter of a particular colour and strength to bring it back to normal. Even so, these things have to be checked, even if only to see that they conform to your personal preference. It would be a very unwise photographer who went ahead with an important session without checking that his film was going to behave in the way he required, or expected.

Once exposed film leaves the photographer's hands and goes to the processing laboratory, there are several other things that can go wrong: it can be lost; suffer incorrect development, or some other processing disaster; come back with strange and unexplained markings on it; or equally strange but easily explained marks such as fingernail snags in the emulsion. It is only fair to say that most laboratories take the utmost care of film while it is in their possession; after all, their reputation is at risk, but accidents can and do happen – usually, again, at the worst possible time! As with checking batches of film – it would be an unwise photographer who allowed all the film he had taken on a job to be processed at the same time. The usual procedure is to divide the film up into sections, allowing one section to be processed and examined before going on to the next. In this way, if something should go wrong, all the film will not be affected.

In the studio, ideas can be *considered, sets can be built, and altered, to suit exactly the requirements of the shot; props can readily be hired or bought, the correct angles for lighting and for a particular idea can be worked out and so on, as in the carefully arranged subject* top left. *This is not to suggest that studio work is easy, far from it; it has its own problems, but it does require a different approach from location work, where picture-making possibilities have to be recognised and used quickly.*

Not every location shot requires props, of course. Sometimes the quality of the light is enough to provide the rich colouring of, for instance, the evening shot of Linda *top centre, or the soft, ethereal feeling of the picture of Tina* top far right, *which was taken on a overcast day in Grenada.*

The balcony of a hotel in Minorca was used for the subject right. *The idea was simple enough and the lack of colour in the setting suggested the bright, colourful outfit of the model, and the happy, carefree pose.*

The shot of Susan facing page, bottom, *was also taken on an assignment in Minorca. The fairly low Mediterranean sun provided the warm, rich light and the shadow patterns.*

Filters are useful accessories, *particularly the skylight, neutral density, and colour-correcting varieties. Ordinary colour filters, as used in black and white photography, can also be used to achieve an over-all colour, when required, as in the shot of Mike and Chekkie above. As with many other optical accessories, however, care needs to be exercised in their use as over-use can tend to be gimmicky and tiresome.*

Problems

Another, quite different problem, is the art director who has dreamed up the shots he wants and supplied a layout without realising – or understanding – the restrictions that photography imposes. To try to explain to a photographically uninitiated art director that he cannot have the product photographed that size, in close-up, and also the model, both rendered pin-sharp, when she is to be lying on a beach a hundred yards away if the correct scale is to be obtained is by no means easy. Unfortunately, there is the occasional art director who feels that as he is paying the money he wants what he wants, and he is not interested in how you do it, or how possible it is. Such an attitude means having to talk the person round to a completely different angle, making them believe that this will produce a nicer shot and, most important, trying to convince them that it is all their idea.

Art directors occasionally expect you to take pictures in someone else's style. They show you a photograph taken by another photographer and say: 'That's the sort of effect I want.' The only answer to this is to explain that that is another photographer's style, not yours, and if that particular style was wanted, then that photographer should have been engaged. Most art directors will understand in the end, but misunderstandings like this can cause delays.

Then there are the times when, arriving at the airport to meet up with a group of people, sometimes up to ten individuals, all ready to go on a trip abroad, one person – often, unfortunately, a model – arrives too late and misses the 'plane. This means that alternative arrangements have to be made for that one person to travel on the next available flight, time is wasted and tempers are frayed. It is not unknown for a model to get lost in the airport itself, or be too busy buying oddments to notice the time, and the result is the same: the flight is missed. The only lesson to be learned from this is that you have to keep an eye on everyone all the time and insist, as far as is possible, that the group keeps together.

Once on location there is the very real problem, as has been mentioned elsewhere, of taking great care that the models do not become too sunburnt or suffer from insect bites.

Wide-angle lenses and *unusual viewpoints, together or separately, can create problems with distortion. In such cases it is preferable to make the distortion obvious as in the shot* above.

Proprietary multi-coloured filters are readily available but many photographers prefer to use squares of coloured gelatine, holding parts of one, two or three over the lens to produce the effect they want; particularly to add colour to a sunless picture below left.

A filter that darkens or changes the colour of only part of the picture can sometimes be used to telling effect. For the shot below, *the photographer, having chosen the black eye-shade and the black bikini and accessories for his dark-haired model, wanted to darken the top area of the picture to add weight and drama. A square neutral density filter positioned across the top part of his lens achieved the effect he wanted. The eye-shade, incidentally, removed any problem that might have been apparent by the model having to half close her eyes against the strong sunlight.*

It would be a pity to shoot only beautifully arranged pictures unless, of course, they are specific fashion shots. People do rush into the sea, their hair gets wet, they look untidy and they have to screw their eyes up against the light, and providing this is what the photographer wishes to convey, these apparent faults can be used, as in the picture, seemingly happy and spontaneous, of Anne Grey right. (All pictures shot on Hasselblad cameras)

61

Advertising

Advertising photography, especially when it requires that a specific brief is closely followed, can be challenging, full of problems, time-consuming, difficult to cost or, rarely, straightforward and simple.

The first the photographer will usually know of it is when the 'phone rings and an art buyer for an advertising agency asks for a quotation for a particular job. After discussing all the various aspects and trying to get the feel of exactly what the agency wants, the photographer has to sit down and carefully work out the quote as best he can; a process that can prove very difficult without knowing exactly how long the model or models will be required for, and how long the retouching or artwork will take to complete. However, the approximate quote is put in writing and, if it is accepted, a meeting is set up involving the photographer, the art director, copy writer, account executive and, perhaps, the client, so that the job can be discussed fully, ideas pooled and problems aired.

In the case of the work shown here, the idea for a series of such ads was initially conceived, jointly, by the art director and the photographer. A decision was made to proceed with one of the ads so that it could be completed and allow everyone concerned to approve or disapprove. The idea for 'Warlord' was chosen and a casting session was then arranged so that the art director and photographer could choose a suitable model. It was considered essential that the girl who was chosen should have the right look for the idea of a science fiction warlord – modern, stormy, sexy, dark haired and with an ability to look slightly aggressive. After seeing some fifty girls one was chosen who fitted the visualised idea and who was also tall enough not to look out of proportion against the motor cycle. She was booked for a half day's shooting and was asked to arrive at the studio without make-up as this would be applied by the make-up artist – the next member of the team to be booked. The make-up artist was chosen for his ability to use his imagination in creating the science fiction look without,

The sketch above was not, as might be thought, produced after the event; it is quite genuinely one of the drawings that were made before any shooting started. About the only difference between it and the finished result, however, apart from the flowing cape, is the lightning in the background of the drawing which does not appear in the final work. It could have been included, but it was felt that it might draw attention away from the motor cycle, and as it was the machine that was being featured it was thought better, instead, to choose a strong colour for the background. Although the idea was only a sketch at this stage, several other drawings had also been made and discussed during meetings between the art director and the photographer, so quite a lot of work had already been done on the project.

The shot of the girl actually on

the motor cycle is not the one that was finally chosen, as is clear from an examination of the finished result. Several slight changes of posture were adopted during the session and it was not until prints had been made that one could be chosen.

The particular motor cycle featured was a big machine, but it would have looked impossibly large had a small girl been chosen for the modelling. This was another factor to be considered in addition to the right look, the right hairstyle

and the right outfit.

The combination of ideas, photography, styling and artwork all finally came together in the finished picture right, which now lacks nothing except the advertising copy at the bottom.

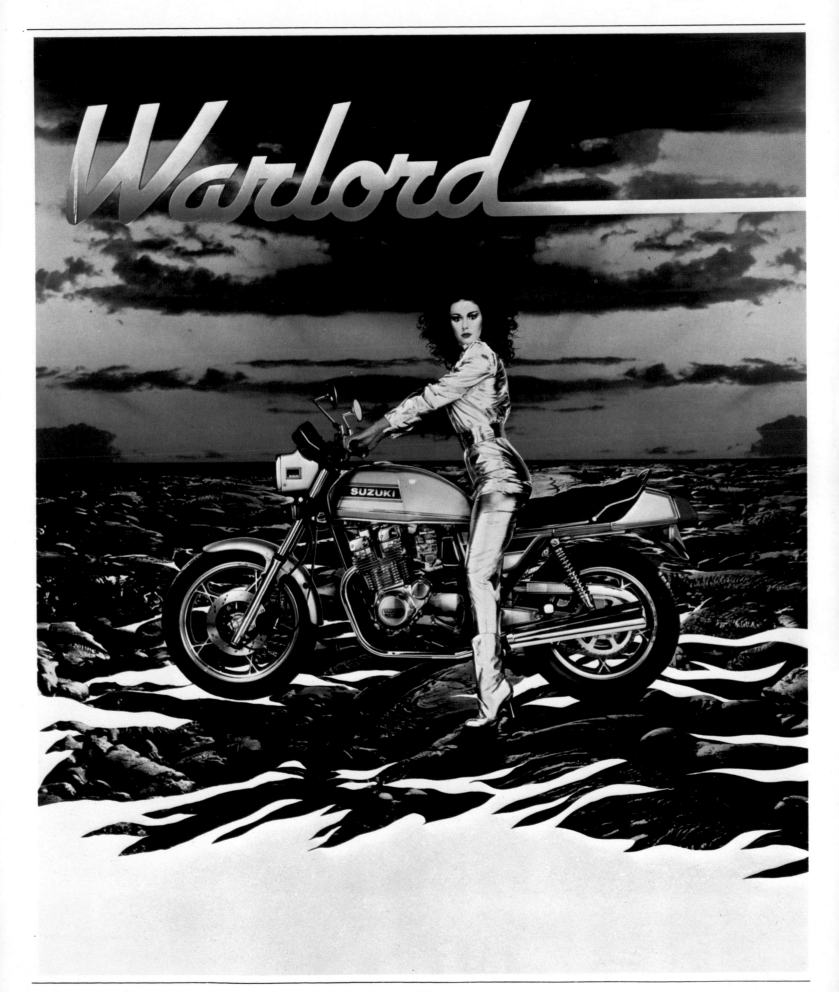

Advertising

however, going too far. The look that was required was discussed with him so that he knew exactly what was expected and would arrive at the studio with the appropriate silver make-up.

The next person to be alerted was the stylist. She was called in for a meeting so that she could be briefed on the outfit which, it was decided, should be silver in colour and consist of a boiler suit with a 'space' look about it. The stylist spent a day getting together about three outfits from which the art director and photographer could choose, together with a selection of boots, gloves, belts and jewellery – none of which would necessarily be used, but which would be on hand just in case.

The bike was then delivered to the studio and, as it had been decided that the shots would be taken and then cut out, in colour print form, from the background, it was set up on a white paper background. A decision had also been made to use electronic flash to light the shot in order to show as much detail in the bike as possible but the girl also had to be properly lit and, as the right lighting for the machinery would not necessarily be ideal for the girl, or vice-versa, a compromise lighting set up had to be arranged.

When the model arrived there was considerable discussion before her make-up was completed, her hair styled and she was able to put her outfit on. Once she was in position on the motor cycle a number of clips were used to pull the outfit in to create a better line, and these were obviously fixed on the far side of the model, away from the camera. A wind machine was placed in position, in case it was decided that a wind-swept look was required.

Once an exposure reading had been taken, using a flash meter, a preliminary Polaroid was made so that all concerned could check every detail – and the photographer could, in addition, check his lighting and exposure. Then, following minor adjustments, several more Polaroids were exposed until everyone was completely happy with the result. The Polaroid back was then exchanged for a film magazine and the actual session started, with make-up artist, hairdresser, art director and photographer's assistant looking on from as near to the camera position as possible – without getting in the way of the photographer – so that they could see approximately what the camera was seeing, in case of any changes in the set-up which would require their

This is one of the series of shots facing page, *taken in the Caribbean for Silhouette Swimwear, for use in their advertising.*

The photographs above *and* left *are part of a series with a sporting theme, shot for the* Fabergé *range of men's toiletries.*

A hair stylist and a make-up artist, as well as the photographer, collaborated to produce the startlingly beautiful but unusual shot top.
(All pictures these pages: Hasselblads)

Advertising

attention. A large mirror was also placed at the camera position so that the model could see herself and check her movements.

When the session was finished and every possible, and desirable, variation within the fairly tight requirements had been shot, the film was sent off to the processing laboratory for a clip test to be made. Once this had been approved the go-ahead was given for all the film to be processed, following which the photographer and art director chose the most suitable transparency for use in the final advertisement. In this particular case a separate background transparency had to be used; this could have been a shot already in the photographer's files, or the agency's, or it could have been shot specially, but in the end it was decided that a suitable shot could be obtained from a stock colour library. The two transparencies – the background and the selected shot from the session – were then made into large colour prints; two to three times the size of the intended advertisement. These large prints were next handed over to a retoucher whose job it was to mount the background print onto stiff board, carefully cut out, by hand, the print of the model and bike and mount it in position on the background. Expert retouching and air-brushing added the finishing touches, after which it only remained for the lettering to be added to the final work so that it could go to the agency for approval and then on to the printer.

Photography has in common with many other professions its 'Catch 22' situations. A photographer may want to do advertising work and be full of ideas but, unless an agency is prepared to take a chance on an unknown, he is likely to be asked to show evidence of advertising jobs he has already worked on. It is little use explaining that, as yet, he has no published work to show, but he wants to produce some and would like to be given the opportunity; most agencies really cannot afford to take risks with valued clients. It is, obviously, possible to break the circle, but it is by no means easy. One way is to shoot pictures that show your expertise – without which you will stand no chance at all – and your ability to come up with new ideas.

Even when a photographer is established there will probably be things he would like to do that are outside the field for which he is known, and it is a common mistake to classify photographers, assuming that, because they earn their living taking, for instance, fashion pictures, this is the only kind of photography they can do. Most photographers wish to expand their horizons; they want to prove – even if only to themselves – that they can do other things in photography. The one attribute they must possess, of course, is a love of photography; a love of creating images; of solving technical problems.

Only one of the pictures on these pages was shot for a specific client, as a commission; that shown facing page, centre right, which was taken for Silhouette, for a lingerie advert. All the rest were taken either for similar reasons to those already discussed, or simply to try out ideas.

(Pictures top *and* facing page, top: Nikon. All others: Hasselblads)

67

Advertising

This New York taxi has been shown earlier but it was felt that it might be interesting to show a few of the other shots that were taken during the same session. The two models, Mandy and Debbie, were provided with a variety of outfits, some matching and some contrasting with the bright yellow of the vehicle. The shots were all taken for the company which owns the cab, for possible use in their own publicity brochure as well as for possible sale to their own clients. As often happens with a session such as this, with no art director involved and with the photographer, Peter Barry,

given very much a free hand – although ideas on how the cab could be used had been considered – one shot led to another until it was felt that all possibilities, within the limits of just the girls and the cab, had been covered.
(All pictures shot on Hasselblads)

Editorial Photography

Editorial photography provides the photographer with an excellent opportunity to take really creative pictures of girls, as there are normally no layouts or directives, as there are in advertising photography. Consequently, when a magazine or newspaper commissions a photographer to produce a few pages of editorial fashion pictures, although they might suggest a theme, or a feeling they would like to see in the spreads, they are more than likely to leave the rest up to the photographer, who can go away and interpret their suggestions in any way he wishes.

The final result – the pages of a magazine or newspaper – inevitably features the girls and clothes looking glamorous and perfect. The methods used in the studio to achieve this perfect look, however, are often far from glamorous. Most of the garments that are to be photographed, for instance, do not fit the model perfectly. A dress may need taking in at the waist, and this is normally done by pulling the material on the side of the girl that is away from the camera, and then securing it with either a hat pin or a safety pin, or clipping it together with a large bulldog clip. If the hem of the garment does not hang straight and even, small lead weights, which have a bent pin attached to them, can be hooked inside the hem, keeping it in position. If it is required that the dress should look as though it is blowing in the wind, and a wind machine would make the dress look too untidy, then a length of nylon fishing line can be knotted and threaded through the hem and tied to a stand, thereby pulling the dress out to one side. The nylon line, being virtually transparent, will not normally be picked up as an image by the camera.

The cameras that are commonly used for editorial photography are 6×6cm or 35mm, usually fitted with motor drives or power winders. Such items are generally considered particularly

Pictures that epitomise the ideas of peace and tranquillity; in which we can experience a certain nostalgia – perhaps for something we have never actually experienced ourselves – are still in demand, both for editorial use as well as for commercial purposes. It is not enough, however, merely to dress a model in the sort of clothes that match this idea and simply shoot pictures of her. The setting, the mood, the choice of colours, the accessories and the photographer's treatment, all have to be brought together if successful shots are to be taken. Soft focus, as used in the picture of Spot above, plus softening around the edges of the frame to suggest a dream-like quality, as in the shot of Leslie left can all help to create this vitally important mood. (All pictures taken using Hasselblad equipment)

Editorial Photography

desirable as the girls both like, and are required, to move constantly and some form of power drive is a great help in keeping up with them.

Although some photographers prefer to keep their cameras fitted to tripods almost permanently, providing you are shooting in the studio, with a fast-recycling electronic flash, or outdoors using a fast shutter speed – 1/125 of a second or faster – then it is better to hand-hold the camera so that you have greater mobility and freedom to change camera angles, rather than ending up with lots of pictures that all look the same.

Alongside a fashion photographer's camera case will usually be found a box containing pins, hat pins, double-sided adhesive tape (useful for sticking hems up and the ends of belts down) weights, scissors, a scalpel (for removing the odd thread from a garment, or cutting the stitching along a seam) nylon thread, tissue paper and cotton wool (for filling out sleeves or trouser legs to make them look smooth).

The financial side of editorial fashion work is always arranged by the magazine or newspaper concerned as they pay both the photographer and the model a set rate, depending on the space that the pictures will occupy in the publication. Although the rates for this work are considerably less than that paid for other kinds of girl photography, photographers are still keen to do it as it affords a show-case for their work, it being normal practice for the photographer to receive a credit under his pictures, and the publication being seen by many potential clients means that he will, hopefully, obtain more work as a result.

Sun, sand, sea and beautiful people; most photographers' dream, it might be thought. Certainly, trips to exotic places have their compensations, whether they are undertaken for editorial work, advertising, or whatever. The very ingredients that provide the attractions – the sun, sand and sea – do, however, create their own problems. The first, and most critical, is that of excessive contrast, leading to dark, heavy shadows. With static subjects such as those right and below this can be overcome to a large extent by the use of fill-in flash or, more commonly, by the use of reflectors to bounce light back into the shadows. Another method is to get the model to lie down, as in the picture left. Incidentally, notice how, in this shot, a graduated filter has been used to darken the sky, and how the inclusion of the

passing couple, unaware that they were being photographed, has added interest and completed the composition.

The next problem, particularly in windy conditions or when shooting close to the water's edge, where there may be considerable natural spray – or you may have asked the models to splash water around to add movement to the picture – is corrosion. Salt spray and sand are deadly enemies of any fine mechanical and optical equipment and when shooting in conditions where either are present it is essential to protect cameras and lenses as much as possible. In addition to nightly cleaning, UV filters on the lenses will not only help protect them but will also assist in cutting down on excess blue in the light. *(Pictures left, below and facing page, bottom: Hasselblads)*

Editorial Photography

Sometimes conditions dictate the equipment that is used for a job. The only way the shots left and below could be taken was by using a lens of over 350mm on the 6 x 6 format – which was not available – or a 200mm lens on the 35mm, which was the camera used. For the picture below, the photographer also used a green gel with a hole cut in the centre, over the lens.

The other pictures on these pages were all seen and taken spontaneously. Sometimes things happen to look right for only a moment; usually unposed, they may be models simply walking away from a location that has just been used. Indeed, if the shot of Kathy top far right had not been taken when the field of flowers was first seen it would have been too late; hours later the field was ploughed. (All pictures facing page: Hasselblads)

The almost unreal blue of the Caribbean Sea and the pattern created by sunlight on the waves made the perfect setting for the shot of Jane Sumner on the airbed facing page. With subjects like this a polarising filter can be useful to reduce reflections should they prove a distraction.

A very simple composition right *has been turned to good effect by the use of strong colour in the lower, empty part of the picture.*

Balloons are useful props to take on a trip. They occupy little space until inflated, they are cheap, and they can be combined to add strong colour above *to produce a happy shot typical of those seen in most holiday travel brochures.*

Not quite so likely to be encountered is the sheer elegance and sophistication of Nina Carter left, *photographed in Sidi Bou Said, Tunisia.*

A very wide-angle lens was used for the picture of Denise Denny top left *in order to obtain sufficient depth of field to show the sand texture in the foreground as well as rendering the background sharp.*

(Pictures top left and above: Pentax 6X7's. All other pictures: Hasselblads)

Erotic Photography

It is important to realise that what is erotic need by no means be distasteful. The problem is in defining just what we mean by erotic. We are all individuals and we all have our own likes and dislikes, and what one person may find very alluring, sexy, titillating, erotic – call it what you will – may well leave another person quite unmoved.

It is fair to say, however, that in order to produce an erotic series of pictures it is not necessary that they should be obvious or explicit. The answer probably lies in subtleties and suggestion; a girl dressed in white underwear may be the sort of thing we would encounter in any of dozens of adverts, but if she is pictured in the same clothing outdoors, at night, the picture takes on a different aspect and meaning. Given a crowded beach with dozens of girls, all wearing bikinis and swimsuits, it is a fair bet that if a fully dressed girl walked by and her skirt blew over her head, then she would suddenly be the focus of a lot of attention. The reason? Probably that we are seeing something that is totally unexpected and that we are not supposed to see. And yet that particular girl would probably be showing far less than all the girls on the beach; therefore it would seem that it is not just what is seen but how it is shown that attracts. It follows that it is no good simply booking a model, asking her to take her clothes off, and expecting to be able

An old, abandoned building provided just the right setting for these pictures of Nina Carter, photographed by Peter Barry in Tunisia. For the shots he had in mind it was essential to find somewhere as deserted as possible and this particular structure also gave him the colour tones he was looking for. The light-coloured, flaking walls acted as reflectors and there were also a number of doors and windows to add to the picture-making possibilities, as well as the badly-eroded surfaces of the building which provided the ideal texture to contrast with the smooth skin of the model.

Before shooting in such a location it is wise to have a good look round it, to make sure that it is, indeed, as uninhabited as it appears, and before asking the model to pose it is also prudent to look inside the building to ensure that there are no non-human residents!

Once a model knows she can trust a photographer not to take shots that she would not like shown, then she will usually co-operate to the utmost in helping to produce an interesting session.

(All pictures taken on Hasselblad cameras)

Erotic Photography

to show a series of erotic pictures as a result. All you will end up with is a set of pictures of a girl without her clothes on. The key to erotic photography is ideas, and it is a subject that probably requires more thought than any other.

Use of lenses

One of the most flattering lenses to use is a medium telephoto; say the 150mm on 6 × 6cm, or the 105mm on 35mm, as these lenses slightly flatten the image and give a very pleasing perspective, especially in body shots. If you want to enhance the look of a girl's legs you can still use the long lens, providing you keep the camera back parallel to the legs, thus avoiding the effects of obvious foreshortening. If you want to make her legs appear longer and slimmer, then it is best to use a moderate wide-angle – nothing of shorter focal length, though, than, say, a 35mm lens on a 35mm camera, or a 50mm on 6 × 6 – as anything shorter than this can cause very obvious distortion. Even with medium wide-angle lenses great care must be taken to choose the right angle and keep distortion to a minimum.

Many – though not all – the photographs that come under the heading of 'erotica' are taken speculatively. This is quite understandable; it is difficult to know, in advance, whether an idea translated into photography will appear erotic or not. The borderline between the acceptable and the unacceptable is, anyway, difficult to decide on until we have something in front of us on which to make a judgement.

All the pictures on these pages were taken speculatively, but they have all subsequently been used for a variety of purposes including calendars, posters, magazines and books. (All pictures: Hasselblad cameras)

Erotic Photography

Erotic photography, like any other kind of photography, requires constant experiment. The market for such pictures constantly demands new models, new ideas and new techniques. There is no point at all in simply asking a girl to take her clothes off and then wondering what sort of pictures to take; the ideas have to be there. We all have our own fantasies, and this is really the art of the erotic; to strike a chord in the viewer that makes him or her view a picture as erotic. Strangely, pictures of nudes are seldom considered as sexy as those in which the

model is wearing some form of clothing, and this, too, indicates, surely, that eroticism is as much in the mind as the eye.

The picture top left *came about as a result of experimenting with lighting tubes. Both Viva's and Tacha's bodies were oiled to obtain the shiny look.*

The ideas for the subjects facing page *and* above *were sparked off by someone seeing the plastic raincoats and suggesting that, being transparent, they would make ideal wear for such shots. The picture left was also an experiment in the use of plastic material.*

(All pictures: Hasselblad cameras)

Erotic Photography

Lighting

It is best to light a girl with very soft, even light, and to position it directly in front of her and above the camera lens so that it casts a small shadow beneath her nose. If you are setting up lighting mainly for her body then a light angled from the side is better, but it should still be soft and even. An effective way to light just the body is to over-light the background – remembering not to under-light the subject – so that light spills from behind, onto her body, outlining all the curves and emphasising the roundness of the breasts.

By placing a mirror below the girl's face and the light directly above, as already explained, the lips can be given an extra highlight, which makes them look very glossy and sexy. The same technique will also produce an extra catchlight in the eyes, adding sparkle and really bringing them to life.

A few tips

Asking the model to lift her arms up will greatly improve the shape of her breasts, but she cannot, of course, keep them in that position for every shot. Always be careful not to allow the model's legs to point towards the camera as this will cause ugly distortions. Under-exposure can, in the right setting, add an air of mystery to a shot, and baby oil gives the skin a healthy sheen. Regarding baby oil – don't be afraid to put plenty on, but it must be rubbed well in, otherwise the model will simply look oily. After applying the oil, try spraying the girl's skin with water; this really makes the droplets stand out.

Eroticism is very much a subjective term. There is really no way of knowing whether something that we find erotic will prove so to most other people; they may find it uninteresting or even distasteful. Each individual photographer will, naturally, have his own ideas on the subject but it is his job to be

aware of current thinking; the fads or trends and, of course, the degree of public acceptance or disapproval at a particular time. Whilst none of the pictures in this section can reasonably be considered blatant, the motor-cycle shot below left *and the picture* right are very much products of their time; such fashions were not even seen until relatively recently. All the photographer has done is to take current fashion ideas and, for want of a better term, 'eroticise' them. The look of the model, however, has to match the style of the clothes, as does her make-up and hairstyle.

By contrast, the shots above and above left are very much in the traditional style. They both feature sexy underwear and the obligatory stockings and suspenders – very much a part of male fantasy. Which of these styles is considered the more erotic must remain a personal choice.
(Picture above left: Hasselblad. Other shots: 35mm SLR's)

Erotic Photography

The soft, luminous lighting on Nina *left was purely that coming through the window, with only the walls of the room to act as reflectors. The picture was taken on location in Tunisia, as were all the other shots of Nina this page.*

A film set in Jugoslavia provided the setting for the picture of Patsy right, its erotic quality emphasised by the fact that she is dressed completely in white.
(All pictures: Hasselblads)

Erotic Photography

None of the pictures on these pages could be considered particularly revealing, and yet there can be little doubt that most people would classify them as sexy, erotic, call it what you will. Whilst it in no way lessens their appeal – indeed, it increases their air of fantasy – they are all obviously contrived situations, the only exception being the shot of Stephanie, facing page, bottom centre in which she is apparently painting her nails, and we get the impression that she might just not know that the camera sees up her skirt. This, too, is the art of the erotic; glimpses of that which we would not normally see, with the model seemingly unaware.
(All pictures shot on 35mm SLR's)

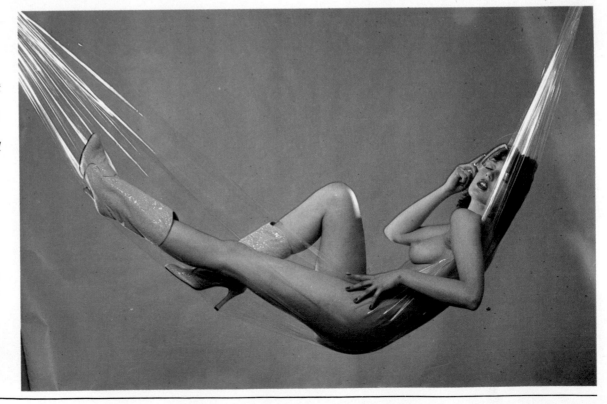

The idea for the picture of Jane Warner left *was not for a sexy shot but was an advert commissioned for Silhouette lingerie. Peter used a soft focus technique and a setting that echoed the rather Edwardian look of the garments Jane was modelling and the result was this charmingly provocative subject.*

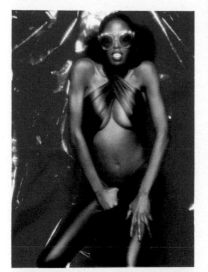

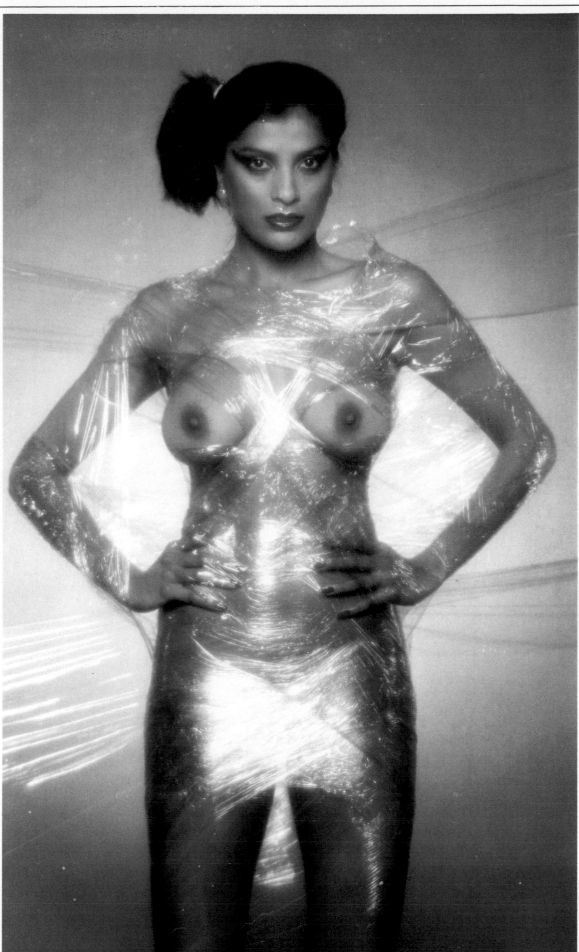

Plastic used in various ways. For the shot of Carol top Peter used red plastic sheeting as a background and dressed her in tight-fitting leather trousers and top. When shooting Nina above he laid black plastic sheeting over a bench, used baby oil to produce a sheen, and got her to pose in red briefs and stockings. The picture of Viva right was rather more involved as it necessitated the use of a considerable amount of cling film carefully wound around her body, leaving her breasts bare. Where the film crossed over itself it became highly reflective and produced this interesting effect. (All pictures taken on Hasselblad cameras)

The Back-up Team

Assistants

These invaluable members of a photographic team are either employed permanently by the photographer, or they operate on a freelance basis. In either case, being an assistant to an established photographer is a time-honoured and, indeed, ideal way for anyone to learn the photography business. Assistants are usually thrown in at the deep end, and they have to cope – or quickly learn to cope – with cameras, lighting, exposures, lenses, looking after clients, keeping models happy, arranging lunches, processing film, hiring or obtaining props, and so on. One of the most important requirements of an assistant, and one that has to be mastered very quickly, is the ability to load and unload a camera, or back, speedily and accurately, without making any

mistakes. This takes the pressure off the photographer and allows him to keep up a rapport with the model, shooting continually so as not to interfere with the mood. A really good assistant eventually learns to anticipate the photographer's needs and wishes, so that when a freshly loaded magazine, or filter, is called for, he is already on hand with it, but this is something that takes time and requires an intimate knowledge of the way in which a particular photographer works.

Make-up Artists

These days more and more photographers use the services of make-up artists as an integral part of a photographic session. This was not always the case, however, and a number of years ago

Fashion assignments can be likened in some ways to film production. A photographer cannot simply arrive, with models and crew, and start shooting. The first thing he will usually do is hire a vehicle and drive around the location – in this case, for Silhouette swimwear, the island of Antigua – looking for settings for the shots he has in mind, making notes as to what will be done where, and so on. Meanwhile, the models will be left to start getting a tan – but with strict instructions not to stay in the sun too long and get burnt. Props have to be chosen, clothes sorted out, and some sort of shooting schedule considered. For the picture right a louvred door was used, which was painted red, and a local helper was engaged to create a hairstyle typical of the area.

(All shots: Hasselblads)

92

models were expected to apply their own make-up. One of the drawbacks of this situation was that each model tended to look the same all the time, as they applied their make-up in the same way each time they visited a studio. Fortunately, models can now look completely different every time they are photographed, as each make-up artist will see them in a different way for each different assignment. Make-up has also become, over the years, much more fashion conscious, and new colours and looks are constantly being created.

A make-up artist will usually bring to a session a wide range of make-up in all colours, together with brushes, remover pads, cotton wool, tissues, nail varnishes and cleansing creams. Ideally, the artist should possess an ability not only to follow the

photographer's direction regarding the type of look required, but also to bring some imagination and flair to the job and suggest ways of improving the look and feeling that is wanted for the shot.

Make-up artists should always have available to them a large, good quality mirror surrounded by either fluorescent strip lighting or bare light bulbs, to light the model's face with a soft, even light; a high stool, so that it is not necessary to stoop over the model for long periods, and, of course, towels as well as a robe for the model to wear while she is being made up.

Well applied make-up takes time and should not be rushed. If a superb result is expected, then there is no substitute for patience. A fairly straightforward facial make-up can take at least one, and possibly two hours to complete, and an expertly applied body

The Back-up Team

make-up may require six hours.

Hairdressers

Hairdressers are normally expected to arrive with, in addition to the obvious combs brushes and scissors, heated rollers, crimpers, coloured hair sprays, and a selection of ribbons, flowers and jewellery to help dress the hair. Professional models will allow their hair to be styled, but they will not usually permit cutting in any way except, obviously, for the odd hair that stands out against a plain and well-lit background, spoiling a smooth hair line.

Stylists

Generally speaking, the best stylists are those who are very experienced, as only through experience can they become known by all the various suppliers, shops, stores and prop hire establishments. Such recognition means that they are respected and trusted to act professionally in seeing that whatever has been borrowed or hired is returned – on time and in the same condition in which it was received. This is vital, especially in the case of valuable items or, for instance, a white dress that will be returned to stock as new.

There are various kinds of stylists. First there is the fashion stylist, who will either obtain entire outfits for the photographer, or just the accessories to match and complement the outfits he has been given to photograph. This particular expert must have a really up-to-the-minute fashion sense, be able to anticipate trends in fashion, and have an ability to memorise colours in order to choose accessories that will perfectly match the outfits the photographer has been given. Second are the props stylists, who need expert knowledge of furniture, pottery and fittings in order to supply props for a particular period if required, but they may also be asked to produce anything, from guns to geese, carpets to coffins and works of art to airplanes. Finally, there are the set stylists who can design a studio set for any given style or period, and can then supply all the necessary furniture, curtains, windows, lamps and so on, right down to the appropriate cigarette lighter on the coffee table.

The same door used for the shots on the previous spread was also used for the pictures above and right. The colour had to be changed as, otherwise, all the subjects being of swimwear, they would have looked too similar. For the same reason, the door was used in different positions so that a choice could be made when the shots were assembled for eventual presentation to the client. However experienced a photographer may be he still awaits, usually with a degree of trepidation, a sight of the processed film, and only considers a job completed following this stage. There are so many things that can go wrong all through the process from choosing the right models, accessories, hairstyles, settings, props, equipment, lighting and exposures and, whilst the photographer can control most of these things, far more subjects are taken than needed, to provide alternatives.

On some assignments, those taken to produce general model shots for instance, when the client may be a photographic library, the photographer will often go on location with just an assistant and the models. He usually knows what sort of pictures are wanted but is often given very much a free hand; providing he brings back good, saleable material, everyone is happy.

For an assignment such as the one featured here, for Silhouette, however, the story is rather different. The prime consideration has to be, understandably, that the

clothes must be shown to their very best advantage; they must fit, look comfortable and wearable, and enhance an already beautiful woman. Because of this there will usually be more people in the party. The client – or a representative – may well come along, together with a stylist, and there will almost certainly be an art director for, although all the requirements will have been thoroughly discussed beforehand, no-one can be quite sure if they will all be possible to shoot before the actual location is seen. Quite different ideas may develop on seeing the settings, and these are very much the responsibility of the art director in consultation with the photographer.
(Hasselblad equipment used for all pictures)

The Back-up Team

The whole purpose of a back-up team is to enable the photographer to produce the results he and the client want, whether it be a simple shot of a carefully outfitted and made-up model right and bottom right, or a dramatically lit and coiffeured subject such as that shown top right.
(Pictures shot on Hasselblads)

In an unglamorous setting – a studio changing room – a model carefully applies her make-up above for a session that will almost certainly produce shots that look very glamorous indeed.

A Japanese hair stylist was the client for whom the subjects top, top right and facing page were taken. The hair styles were, therefore, very important. Nevertheless, an over-all look was wanted that projected his ideas, in much the same way that a dress designer seeks a total look.

The hairstyle of the model on the facing page immediately suggested the idea of the puppet and a stylist was engaged to find an outfit, shoes and scarf etc., that carried this idea through. The make-up, too, was carefully designed to create the illusion of a puppet face and the model was positioned to seem as though she was in a toy box; her expression and attitude supplying the finishing touches.
(Picture above: Mamiya RB67; facing page: Hasselblad)

A fog generator was used to create the whisps of smoke in the background of the fashion shot left, produced for a page of the Littlewoods mail order catalogue.

To suggest the strength and protective qualities of Arborite laminate, the suits of armour below were chosen to contrast with the vulnerability of the nude model.

The shot bottom was taken purely as an experiment to show the metallic-looking outfits against the massive metal doors.

The picture of Viva right was shot from directly above so that her hair could be arranged in this particular way which, together with the slight unsharpness of her face, suggest a falling movement.

(All pictures taken on Hasselblad cameras)

Retouching and Airbrushing

There are several different methods of altering the appearance of a photograph, either in the very slightest way – the minimum of retouching – or radically, until the picture no longer resembles the original at all.

Retouching

Firstly, a print or transparency, black and white or colour, can be retouched using a very sharp retouching blade, or scalpel, to scrape away, with very light strokes, unwanted hair lines, blemishes, or the like. Great caution needs to be exercised as only the thinnest surface layer should be removed. Any light areas left by the knife can now be touched in with a very fine brush and retouching inks. It must be emphasised that all forms of retouching require practice, patience and great care. Various chemicals can also be used to achieve the same results, but this is usually a specialised process requiring training and experience.

There are several ways the requirements for the picture below could have been approached. The name of the motorcycle obviously suggests speed, and movement could have been introduced in the photograph of the machine. This, however, would have meant that it would not have shown the detail wanted, so the impression of speed had to be created in the background. A transparency with an abstract pattern of converging lines, that contained the colours wanted, and also had in it the requisite movement, was chosen and a print of this was combined with the studio shot of the girl on the motor-cycle which, together with airbrushing, produced this striking result. Except for the initial photograph of the two models, on which the idea for the futuristic subject right *was based, the whole picture is the product of the imaginations of the photographer and airbrush artist – and the latter's careful workmanship.*

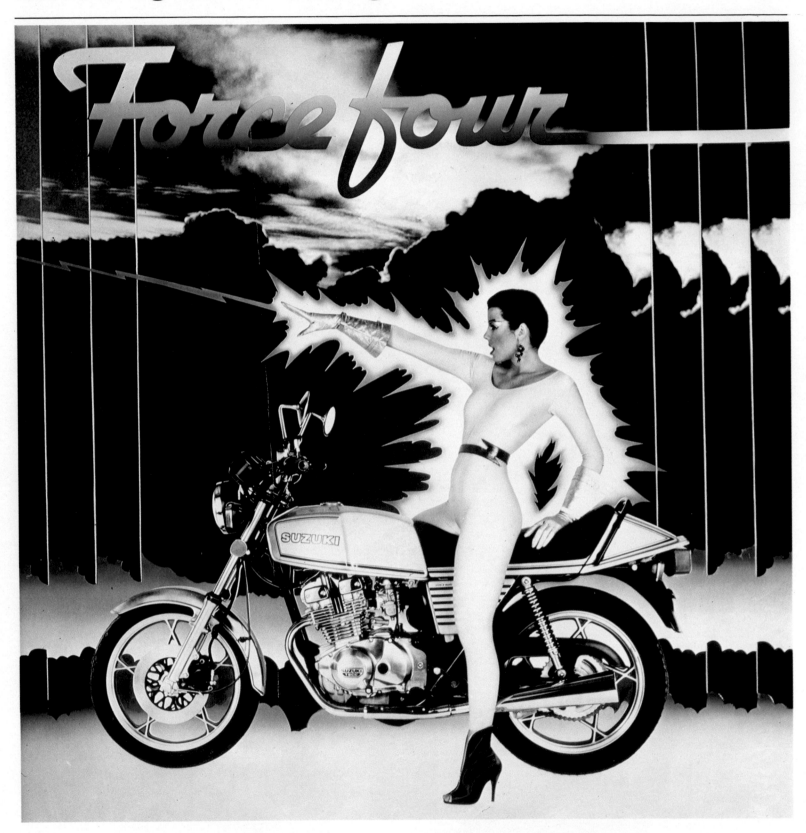

Hand Colouring

Before colour films became readily available, hand colouring of black and white prints was very popular, and was a service that was offered by many photographers. Hand colouring is seldom seen nowadays except to produce a particular effect that attracts simply because it is so unusual, such as leaving most of the print in black and white and only colouring one feature – perhaps the hair, or the eyes, or maybe the lips, or even some other single object that would not normally be considered colourful – to draw attention to the fact that this is not the usual type of print; that things are not always what they seem.

The usual method applied to hand colouring is first to soak the black and white print in clean water, allowing the excess to drain away or removing it with a squeegee. Photographic tints or dyes

Another example of the possibilities of combining artwork, imagination and photography is *shown* facing page.

Make-up need not be limited to its more usual applications. It can be used to create bizarre effects that are still, however,

make-up in the accepted sense top left, *and it can also be used, in the hands of a specialist, to create quite astonishing effects, from the 'sculpture' left to the* models outfit above, *both of which consist solely of make-up applied to the nude models. (All pictures: Hasselblads)*

Retouching and Airbrushing

can then be applied using a fine, camel hair brush. The colour should be used very sparingly, gradually building up more and more colour until the desired effect is achieved.

Toning

Black and white prints can be toned to produce almost any colour, but the effect is now considered too subtle, and a little dated. The method is very simple and does not require a darkroom. A print with good contrast, on matt or semi-matt paper, is the best starting point. This print is placed in a dish of bleaching solution until the darkest tones fade to a washed-out appearance; this usually takes two to three minutes. After washing, transfer the print to a dish containing toner solution where, after only a few seconds it will take on the colour of the toner. Leave it in the solution for about five minutes to allow the colour to reach its full depth before washing and drying the print in the normal way. By using brushes loaded with bleach, water and toner, isolated areas of a print may be toned, a method that can produce some quite unusual effects.

Airbrushing

An airbrush employs compressed air to create a fine mist of paint, dye or ink through an aperture in a pen-like gadget, the whole being on much the same principle as a normal paint spray, but greatly miniaturised. Extraordinary effects can be achieved with an airbrush but it is something that requires a rather specialised technique as well as expert instruction.

Photo montage

This method of altering the final result of a photograph is not, strictly speaking, either retouching or airbrushing, although one or both of these techniques is often employed in producing the final result. The method is quite simple and straightforward in theory but requires great care and precision in execution. It consists of simply cutting out parts of one print – either in black and white or colour, or a combination of both – and sticking them down on another print. As can be seen in the illustrations, the cut-outs can be very simple or complicated and can consist of one image or many. The edges of the cut-out should be touched-in – in colour or black and white as appropriate – so that there is no white edge showing, and the prints should be stuck down with a rubber based mounting adhesive so that they can be lifted and re-positioned if necessary. Once in final position the whole montage should be lit and re-photographed so that the edges and joins do not show.

Make-up alone was used to create the disreputable-looking character facing page. *The photography is straightforward enough; no retouching being required, and by far the greatest part of the credit for its production – apart from the photographer's original idea – must go to the make-up artist Christine Skivens. It was she who translated the idea into reality, first taking a beautiful young model as her canvas, so to speak, and drawing on her body the outlines of the outfit before filling in the colours and then adding the final touches,* notably the scruffily unshaven look. Such make-up cannot be applied quickly; it requires immense patience and care as well as expertise and, indeed, equal patience on the part of the model. All the time the work is in progress – and it can take several hours – she can do nothing but wait, gratefully accepting the odd snack and cigarette!

The pictures right *are part of a series taken by Peter Barry – the photographer of the final result – to show the work as it progressed. (Pictures* right *taken on Nikon equipment. Facing page: Hasselblad)*

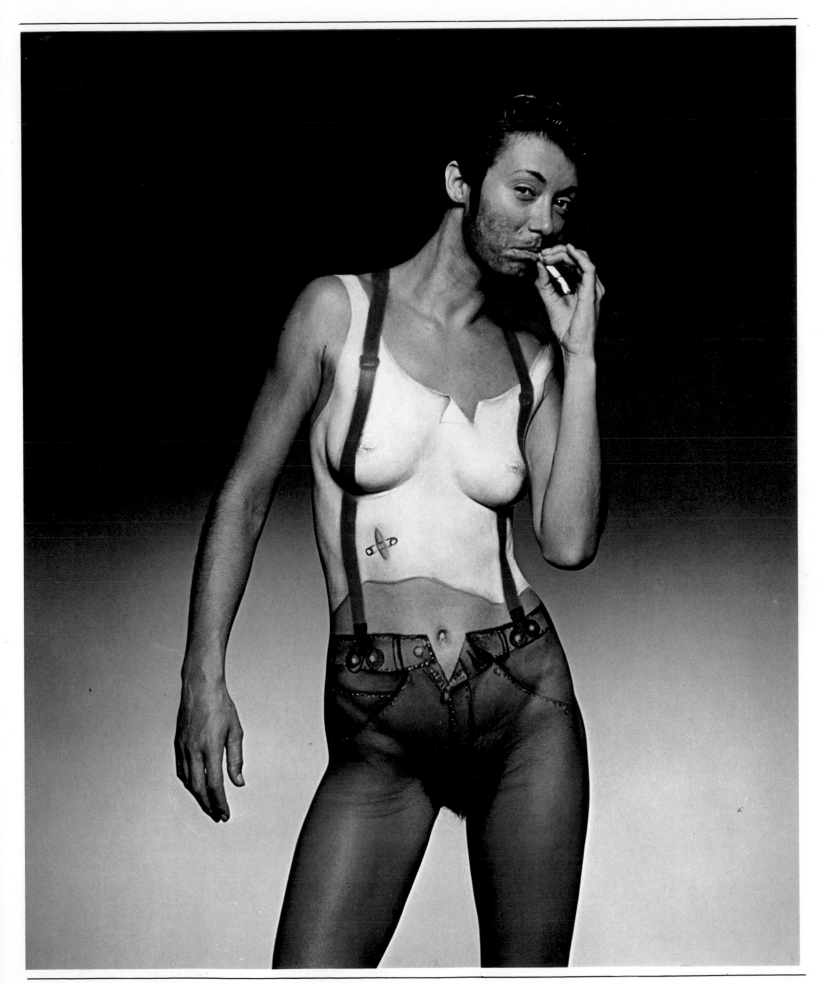

Retouching and Airbrushing

Shown on these pages are some further examples of the sort of imaginative work that can be accomplished by an expert make-up artist.

The ideas using Carol below and Susie facing page *were to photograph the nude body but to suggest that it was, in fact, clothed, whilst creating an air of fantasy.*

For the picture of Viva right silver metallic make-up was used all over, except for the bright red of her lips. It is vitally important, when using any metallic body colouring, to leave an area of skin free and uncovered. Failure to do this will mean that the skin cannot breathe, and this can have very dangerous consequences for the model.

The backgrounds and settings for all these pictures were, of course, chosen to be visually in keeping with the idea of the

different subjects. None, however, more so than the zebra-stripe background used for the picture – again of Viva – bottom right. The idea for this shot is clever and original enough, but the execution – the application of the body colouring and the way it blends with, follows and matches the background, is quite brilliant. The difficulties were considerable: there was obviously no way the model could hold this position for the time required for the colours to be applied, and yet the slightest alteration in position would have destroyed the illusion that model and background were one and the same.

(All pictures taken on Hasselblad equipment)

Some Personal Experiences

In this business, probably because people who are often complete strangers may be thrown together in quite intimate situations for a few hours, days or even weeks, in a strange place; where some of them will be required to pose in bizarre or exotic costume, or none at all, against an extraordinary background, odd situations can arise, and people can sometimes act in strange ways. The following experiences must be considered in context; it would be quite wrong to imply that all sessions or trips are disastrous, or that all models are silly and scatterbrained. Most trips and sessions go off smoothly, or with only the occasional, minor difficulty. Nevertheless, things can go badly wrong, and I am quite sure that other photographers would be able to relate similar events, some amusing and others infuriating.

On one occasion I had arranged a model casting for an advertisement in which a girl was required to wear stocking tights and nothing else – although she would be able to cover her breasts with her arms. Several model agencies were contacted, so that we, the client and myself, could be given a wide choice of models. The requirements were specified. The girls had to have good legs, be willing to model tights and be photographed topless, and they should have long, blonde hair which would, if necessary, cover their breasts. When the girls eventually turned up, however, one girl had black hair, unshapely legs and was not willing to be photographed topless, so both her time and ours was wasted, thanks to her agency not listening to our requirements properly.

Another girl turned up for a session after I had spent all day building a tent out of curtain material. The lighting was arranged, and the idea was that I should take shots of the model climbing out of the tent, as though it was early morning and she had just woken. I asked her to stretch and yawn for a few shots, to emphasise this idea of waking up, to which she replied: 'I don't!' My client asked her: 'You don't what?' 'I don't stretch or yawn,' she replied, firmly. What she really meant was that she did not wish to be photographed in any pose that would in any way detract – in her mind – from her beauty! The client's instant reaction was that we should cancel her booking and get a girl who would go along with our simple request. Unfortunately, however, we were running short of time, so we had to compromise and settle for a much simpler pose. Needless to say, neither the client nor myself have booked that particular model since, and we probably never will.

Then there was the famous model who shared her home with twenty-seven cats. A bed featured in the studio set and, when she discovered two cats seeking warmth under the covers, she promptly joined them, started talking to, and fussing over them, and refused to leave them for an hour, during which time my clients were waiting impatiently! She eventually put in an appearance and from then on she worked like a dream, helping to produce an excellent session.

One girl I worked with lost all her luggage on a flight to Tenerife and arrived with only the casual clothes she was wearing for the flight. She refused to leave her room for several days, until her cases eventually turned up.

I recall numerous girls arriving at airports only to discover that they had not brought their passports. They had to be sent straight home to collect them while other flights were arranged.

For an advertising shot, we once covered a girl from head to toe in grey make-up – except for bright red lips. So taken with it was the model that she decided, after putting on a simple, loose-fitting outfit, that she would go home as she was, to show off the make-up. She travelled home by public transport, no doubt to the amazement of other passengers!

Another girl, made up in a similar way, also decided to go home

All the pictures on these pages feature one model, Nina Carter, and one place – Sidi Bou Said, Tunisia. In addition to showing the obvious charms and versatility of Nina, the shots give a good idea of the numerous interesting locations – providing the photographer recognises their picture-making possibilities – that a new, or 'Different' location provides. Doubtless a Tunisian-based photographer would find our towns and cities, though familiar to us, equally fascinating seen with a fresh eye. (All pictures taken on Hasselblad equipment)

Some Personal Experiences

as she was. She slipped a robe on, got in her car, and made her way home with the intention of surprising her boyfriend by walking in wearing nothing but the startling make-up. Unfortunately she was not aware that her boyfriend had invited other friends for drinks, but she certainly succeeded in creating the surprise she intended!

When on location in Portugal, photographing men's fashions for a magazine, the client and I had great difficulty in finding the right background. Eventually we decided to use some large boulders standing on the beach of a small town near Lisbon. Two of the male models were dressed in swimwear and beachwear, and the two girls – who were there to add some glamour – were in the process of changing into suitable clothing when we all noticed that we were being observed from a cliff high above by about a dozen policemen equipped with binoculars and rifles. We had thought that we were totally concealed among the rocks, and had not realised that there was a police station on the top of the cliff above us. Apparently, the Chief of Police had wandered out for a cigarette, had looked over the cliff and seen the girls undressing, and had called out all the officers to 'observe' for a while before swooping down to arrest us and march us all off to the station. We spent the day in a freezing cold room, in wet clothes and without food or, indeed, contact with the outside world – not a pleasant experience. At the end of the day, just as we had given up hope of being released before the morning, we were bundled into the back of a Landrover and rushed off to a court room in an even colder building where, after listening to the case, which was all conducted, of course, in Portuguese, for some two hours, an interpreter with a singularly unfortunate turn of phrase listened to the summing up and explained that, although the male models and I were cleared, the girls were 'condemned'. This turned out to mean that they were to be fined about £30. We paid the fine and got out as fast as we could – back to the hotel bar and a well-needed drink!

A considerable amount of time seems to be spent just waiting around in this business. Waiting for models to arrive, hair and make-up to be completed and backgrounds to be finished. Sometimes there are other factors that delay shooting, as happened when I was in the South of France. I had been sent there by a cosmetics company to photograph the legendary Brigitte Bardot, but the complicated negotiations between the client and Miss Bardot seemed to have temporarily broken down when I arrived, so I had to wait for a week – at my client's expense – until agreement was reached to allow me to start work. The job was all finished in a day, but I must say that I found 'BB' delightful to work with.

Working with personalities is not always so pleasurable, however. I recall having to photograph a famous racing driver, at the track, for a well-known cosmetics company. He arrived and I was introduced to him and he then announced that I had seven minutes in which to shoot the job! All I could do was to tell him that if he didn't care how he appeared in an advertisement, then why should I? On that occasion I simply had to do the best I could under the circumstances.

At one time I was working in the Seychelles, photographing two girls, together, for a book. We were shooting on a beautiful, secluded beach, miles from any town. I wandered along the beach, looking for a suitable location for the shots, and the girls decided to change on the beach. In my absence, a plain-clothes policeman – dressed in Bermuda shorts and a brightly-coloured shirt – wandered up to the girls almost unnoticed. They were totally naked and he promptly arrested them for indecent exposure, although there wasn't another person to be seen for miles. This time we ended up in court at 8.30 the following

In Barbados, Vicky top was photographed from a low angle to set her against the deep blue of the sky, whilst the rock formations typical of Portugal's coastline were used as the setting for the shot of Jaleh above. Kathy Simmons' lively expression right was captured in Cyprus.

(All pictures: Hasselblads)

Some Personal Experiences

morning, in front of a magistrate who, by 9 o'clock walked out of the courtroom and passed out – apparently from too much alcohol!

On another occasion I had to do a session where the requirement was that the model should be clothed in only a pair of stockings, although her top half could be covered by her arms. A casting session was held, with the clients present, at which we saw some thirty models. We explained the job to each one, and showed them the layouts so that they would understand exactly what was involved. We eventually chose a model and booked her, and on the day of the session she duly arrived and went into the dressing room to put the stockings on. I had my assistant with me as well as the two clients (both of whom were male). The model then came into the studio, onto the plain paper background, and prepared to get into position. I could see straight away that something was wrong; she was not at all happy, so I went over to talk to her, and she told me that she had never done a job like this before, and was really too shy! She could not bear the idea of the two clients watching her, even though I explained – and, indeed, she knew – that this was perfectly normal in advertising photography. Nothing I could say seemed to help and it soon became obvious that we were not going to be able to get the session shot that day, so I told her to go back to the dressing room while I explained the situation to the clients. I did make one more attempt to coax her into doing the job, but she wouldn't, so,

regretfully I had to send her home, without payment. We then had to arrange a second session, using our second choice of model.

Most clients don't really understand situations like this, but it has to be borne in mind that models are not just so much merchandise; they are normal, sensitive human beings. Indeed, I sometimes think that being in the limelight all the time probably makes them over-sensitive. This comes to mind when I remember a model I was using for a fashion shot in the studio. When she arrived she appeared to be perfectly happy, but when we had been shooting for half an hour or so she suddenly burst into tears. I think the client thought at first that I must have said or done something to upset her, but as neither of us could get a word out of her, nor stop her crying, I suggested to the client that he sit down and have a coffee while I took her to a local bar for a drink. After several large brandies, the girl explained that she was in the middle of divorce proceedings and had received, just before the session, a rather unpleasant 'phone call from her solicitor, and the whole thing had suddenly become too much for her. After a further couple of large brandies – which, together with what she had already consumed would, in normal circumstances, have rendered her incapable of walking, let alone working – she brightened up and we went back to the studio and started work again on the session, which turned out to be highly satisfactory.

I was once photographing, in the studio, a group of girls, five in all, in various stages of undress. The art director and the client

An extreme wide-angle lens on the 6X7 format was used for the shot above, *taken in the Grenadines. Such a lens produces marked distortion, particularly if the camera is tilted up or, as in this case, down.*

Poppy fields make irresistible settings. The beautifully-composed subject left *allows us to make our own minds up about the story it has to tell.*

Equally well executed are the pictures facing page, *particularly in their lighting. The props have been used to excellent effect and a soft focus attachment has been added* far right *for a soft, mysterious quality.*

(Picture above: Pentax 6X7. All others 6X6 format but no details available)

turned up – which was fine – but eventually about fourteen other men found their way into the studio and stood behind me, watching the proceedings. At first, one or two of the models objected, but then, when I realised what was happening, I objected most strongly, as they were interfering with the session. I had to explain to the art director that I wouldn't take another shot until everyone who had no business in the studio had left. Within a few moments the studio had been cleared and I was able to carry on with the session. This business does, by its nature, unfortunately attract a number of people who turn up at a session not to help, but to watch.

Weather can prove a problem on location, particularly on overseas trips, where the costs of delays or reshoots are very high. It is, of course, possible to take out insurance against bad weather, and although I have never done this myself, I do know of one or two clients who have done so when long trips abroad were involved. I remember a client coming to me, not so long ago, in a great hurry to get a trip to the Seychelles organised. I set everything up, booked the models, and flew off on my assignment as quickly as I possibly could. I imagined that the client, being so insistent on the Seychelles, would have checked on the weather conditions at that time of the year – January. We arrived to find that it was the middle of the rainy season! Not only that; it was the rainiest rainy season they had experienced in many, many years. I think we had two full days of sunshine out of fourteen. I suppose I

should not have objected to spending two weeks in a beautiful villa in the Seychelles with two lovely girls, but it did matter to me that I got the job done so I ended up shooting most of the sessions in the pouring rain – which certainly looked different – or inside, with hand flash units.

Turkey was the location for a swimwear catalogue I was photographing. The art director and I found a beautiful waterfall with underground caves which we were both very keen to shoot in, but we needed a shaft of sunlight in just the right place in order to make our ideas work. A group of ten of us arrived at the waterfall at about eight the next morning, having driven for an hour over rough, bumpy roads, but the sky chose to cloud over so we had no option but to wait, hoping the weather would clear. We all made our way to a little local bar, from where we could keep an eye on the weather. It was quite a cold morning so we started drinking raki, a local, aniseed-tasting drink. By about nine-thirty that morning we were in no condition to notice weather or, indeed, anything else, and we had to abandon the morning's shoot!

Although the hotels in Turkey were generally excellent, there was one, tucked away in some remote part of the country where we had to spend a few days, that was anything but. When we first arrived we discovered that there was no hot water, which particularly upset the girls. A little while later we found that electricity was available for only a couple of hours a day, and this meant that the models using hairdryers or rollers was out of the

question. Added to this came the realisation that not only was there no hot water, most of the time there was no water at all! The girls were not amused. The final straw – cockroaches and other bugs in the rooms – nearly caused a mutiny. Fortunately, we soon moved on, and went from one extreme to the other when we booked into the Sheraton, in Istanbul.

On my third trip to Tunisia I found that every time the models and I drove to a particular beach, and then dragged bundles of swimwear, equipment and accessories to a suitably lonely, and secluded spot, it would suddenly pour with rain and we would

have to look for shelter, or dash back to the car. It almost seemed that someone didn't want us to work on that beach.

I think I would find it difficult to count the times I have had to shoot swimwear in the winter and fur coats in the summer. Indeed, on one of the hottest summer days, I recently had to photograph a famous boxer and a couple of models in Christmas settings – Father Christmas outfits included. The session lasted all day, and I would imagine that everyone involved must have dropped at least one weight division by the time it was over!

Photographing the Nude

The nude female form has long been a favourite subject for painters, sculptors and photographers. With this subject, probably above all others, it is important that all the elements of the picture: subject, pose, background, lighting and viewpoint are brought together harmoniously and tastefully. Few subjects can be less appealing than a badly photographed, lit or posed nude shot.

If the desired result is a flattering, soft, natural look, then it is really best to use natural light. If outdoors then the subject should be in the shade; if indoors she should be lit by light falling through an open window or door, with a white reflector placed on the side away from the light, to bounce light back into the shadows. Failing such lighting, then electronic flash so arranged as to provide soft, even lighting can be used. An interesting effect can be produced by allowing light to fall on the model through palm leaves or venetian blinds so that the light appears to fall in strips, creating geometric patterns.

Basically, good nude photography must depend on your own ideas and good taste and the main criterion has to be whether it looks right to you. The model, however, should always appear feminine and graceful, with the lines and curves of the body flowing rather than angular. It is worth remembering that the camera tends to make the nude look heavier, so if any part of the girl's figure is rather larger than is ideal, care should be taken with both pose and viewpoint to minimise this. There are good and bad angles for the breasts, waist, hips and thighs, which can only be discovered by constant observation. Remember also that it is often both more erotic – and tasteful – for the model to be either semi-clothed or draped in some way rather than blatantly naked.

Do not be afraid to close right in on the model and shoot just a section of her body; this can make for a very strong, simple shot. At the other extreme the nude can be just a small, integral part of

Karen, photographed on these pages by Beverley Goodway, must surely be most people's idea of an ideal nude model. There is a considerable difference between a model with no clothes on and someone like this, who has no inhibitions about appearing nude but nevertheless manages to retain an air of freshness, vitality and femininity. Lighting is important in all photography, but nowhere is it more so than in the photography of nudes. Ugly shadows, excessive contrast and uneven lighting can quickly spoil a picture. Particularly when all the attention is focused on the model, as here, the backgrounds must also be bright and clean, as must any props or accessories, shoes etc. A bruise or blemish on the skin can turn a beautiful picture

into something tatty and tawdry.

A light reflected into a white umbrella, used a little above and to one side of the camera, and a white reflector to soften the shadows, form a good starting point for lighting shots such as these. Once this basic lighting set-up is fully understood, then other lights can be added, perhaps two or more grouped around the camera, and another lower down, running on half power. (Mamiya RB67 equipment used for all pictures)

Photographing the Nude

the overall design of a picture, and this can be just as telling in its own way.

It is best to avoid legs or knees pointing towards the camera as this can cause ugly distortions. The soles of the feet are best kept out of sight as they are seldom attractive. Even elbows can look ugly, and if the model leans to one side there are bound to be creases – although these can be eliminated, at least in part, by getting her to stretch upwards. Even though such things as elbows and, indeed, creases, are perfectly natural, they can still look unflattering so are best avoided. If the model has wrinkles or other marks on her skin, do use a diffusing filter and slightly overexpose – this will help a lot. The answer to all these problems, if disappointing results are to be avoided, is constant, constant observation of every part of the subject.

Warm skin tones tend to be more pleasing to the eye than cold, blue tones and, as has been mentioned, soft lighting is preferable to hard lighting with its harsh, sharp shadows, although this does not mean that all pictures should be made in only one way. The more 'different' a shot you can produce, through experimentation, the better. Photography and photographic techniques must keep changing – they should never stand still.

Always compliment a model on her best features and refrain from mentioning her worst. This is good for her self-confidence and encourages her to be outgoing and co-operative.

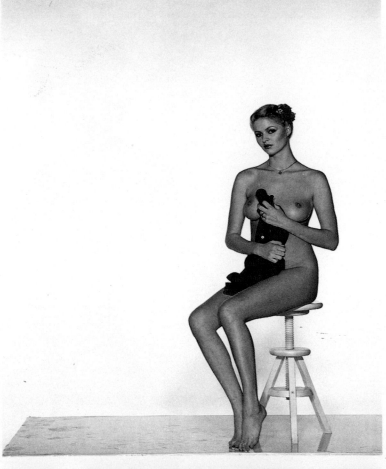

Nude pictures are not necessarily erotic pictures. We see far too much nudity nowadays for it to have the same effect it once did. This is all to the good; it means that the photography – the actual picture – becomes more important, rather than the mere fact that this is a picture of a woman with no clothes on.

Outdoor nude studies are

obviously more difficult, generally, to manage than studio shots. There is not the guaranteed privacy outdoors, and it is therefore difficult for a model to relax to the same extent she can in the studio.

(Pictures above, right and facing page, bottom: Hasselblads. Other pictures: Mamiya RB67's)

Photographing the Nude

The very natural-looking shot
facing page *concentrates all the attention on the model. It was taken using only the soft daylight coming through the window, creating the lovely backlit effect, and the mellowness of the late evening sun matches perfectly the mood of the picture as well as the predominant colour scheme of soft browns, yellows and oranges.*

The blue of the garment Nina
Carter is wearing tones well with the blue ceramic against which she was photographed above. Ceramic tiles are highly reflective, however, and great care should be taken to ensure that the flash is positioned to minimise the effects of flare.

The other three pictures on this page all make use of black backgrounds. Black is excellent for showing up the halo around light hair when it is backlit above left *and even accentuates the effect of a top light* left. *It also outlines the model's body well, and certainly adds a dramatic quality. It is very important, however, that the edges of the subject should not be too dark as, if they are, they can become lost in the background as can, of course, dark hair and clothing.*
(Pictures facing page and above: Hasselblads. All others: Mamiya RB67's)

Nothing is Real

The ideas for the Nothing is Real pictures were conceived by the photographer while studying the work of several artists – including that of Magritte, Dali and Escher. The next consideration was whether it would be possible to combine the fantasy and surrealism of the artists' work with that of the realism of photography. It was decided that the best results would probably be achieved by the use of the photographic image combined with the arts of retouching, airbrushing and photo montage.

Six ideas were eventually decided on and models were booked who were chosen because their looks and figures seemed best to suit the mood and feel of the proposed shots. Each model was then photographed, first in the exact position that had previously been worked out, and then in alternative positions in case the original did not quite work as planned. As it happened, the first shot was fine and was used in every case. Colour prints – 20 × 30 inches – were then made from the transparencies. The large size was considered necessary as it made them rather easier to work on, and by the time they were reduced to book or magazine size, any signs of retouching would be minimal. The next stage was to call in a freelance retoucher/airbrush artist, and the ideas were discussed with him in great detail, using, where possible, tear sheets from art magazines, books and so on, so that he would know exactly the effect that was required. He now mounted the main shot onto stout card and proceeded to cut out the other prints, with a scalpel, and mounted the parts he wanted on the main print, using cow gum or spray mount. The photographer and the retoucher worked very closely together on this stage in order to keep to the original idea. Sometimes it was necessary to strip

It would be pointless to imagine that the seemingly simple, but quite complex to produce, images these pages were within the province of the average photographer. In the first place he or she might well not be interested in producing such subjects, and secondly, they are by no means purely photographic images, but a combination of the skills of the photographer, the printer and the airbrush artist. Nevertheless, they do show what can be achieved using such combined talents.

The subject facing page is, on the other hand, totally photographic. A transparency of one of the figures was projected onto the model and adjusted until the wood grain pattern was the size wanted. The resulting shot was then combined with the shot of the figures and the relative sizes adjusted so that the grain pattern was on an equal scale. (All pictures taken on Hasselblad equipment)

The 'magic carpet' idea left *is easily recognisable as a photograph of a model lying on a carpet, the resulting print of which has had the background added and modified. This is probably the simplest type of treatment combining photography and artwork and would prove the easiest idea to start with in attempting this kind of work. The shot of the head* facing page *is more complex, however, and required a great deal of masking, airbrushing and hand painting to produce the 'peeled orange' effect. With the other subjects* below *and* bottom left *it is difficult to know where artwork begins and photography ends. Apart from the basic shapes photographed, most of the work was completed in the artist's studio.*
(For original photographs: Hasselblads)

everything down and start again. Finally, the completed artwork was rephotographed on colour negative film stock so that further prints could be made should the original be lost or damaged.

Once the six projects were completed they were shown to clients, including a publisher who decided that the ideas could be made into a book, and a further forty-four subjects were commissioned and completed over the next six months. As the photographer worked through the shots, inspiration came from the most unlikely sources: candles, nutcrackers, toothpaste tubes, motor cycles etc., until in the end literally everything became a possible subject to be used in creating unreality!

Nothing is Real

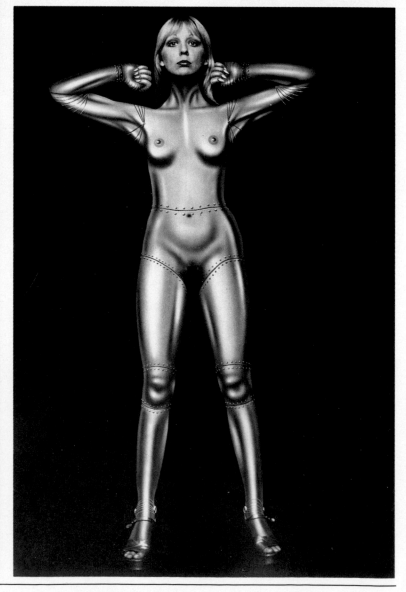

Two of these subjects are straightforward – if such a term can be applied to this kind of picture – in that they are basically one single photographic print in each case, on which the artist has worked. Obviously, the amount of work necessary on the shot right *was relatively small, the basic idea already existed in the photograph and it only required the addition of the puff of air coming out of the model's ear, and the pump, to complete it. In contrast, the picture* below, *although remaining a recognisable nude shot, was completely reworked except for the head, to create the impression of the metal-clad, robot-like body.*

The pictures left *and* bottom left *were produced using, in addition to airbrushing, the montage technique. After working on the shot of the model to produce the 'Superwoman' effect, it was carefully cut out and mounted in position on the print of New York before final touches were applied to the combined prints.*

The cat-woman and moon was the result of combining four different photographic images: the sand, the dried plants, the model and the cat's head all being printed to the required, relative sizes, they were then cut out and mounted together before the background and whiskers were added by the artist.
(All original photographs taken on Hasselblads)

Nothing is Real

Most photographers have at some time taken – if only by accident – double exposures or unusual juxtapositions of images: the setting sun seemingly balanced in someone's hand, people with, apparently, two heads simply because the body of one person hides the body of another, and so on, which have proved interesting because of the air of unreality they displayed. It is a short step from finding such 'accidents' interesting to setting out to take them deliberately, using extreme wide-angle or telephoto lenses, mirrors, double exposures etc., to distort reality. From there we may go on to mounting such transparencies in combination with others to accentuate the effect, or create new ones, or we may try cutting out portions of prints and mounting them on other photographs, or artwork, to make collages. If we get to this stage we will almost certainly be hooked, and probably start investigating the use of artwork and airbrushing to create the new images we want; images such as those shown on this page.

The lovely golden statue effect of a temple dancer involved no artwork whatever, but an immense amount of artistry in the make-up, hair styling and construction of the clothing and props. When this was all done the model was carefully posed against the gold background and lit so as to emphasise the 'goldness' that was wanted.

It is worth repeating that when using metallic body make-up it is vitally important that an area of skin is left unpainted to allow the model's skin to breathe.

Acknowledgments

The publishers express their thanks to W.L. Pawson and Son Limited for permission to use photographs featuring Silhouette swimwear and lingerie, and to Brandmark International Limited for permission to use photographs taken for their clients Fabergé and Suzuki.

In addition to the work of the author, Peter Barry, whose photography accounts for the majority of the pictures in this book, the following photographers are also represented:

Philip Barker
Michael Boys
Marcus Brown
Adam Cole Studios
Ronald Falloon
David Gibbon
Beverley Goodway
Michael Hannau
G. Hitchcock
Murray Irving
David James

Clive McLean
Peter Meech
Peter Pugh-Cook
John Robertson
Roy Round
David Stamford
Neil Sutherland
Manfred Uselmann
Pedro Volkert
Brian Ward
Rosemary Weller

**Designed and Produced by
Ted Smart and David Gibbon**

Published by **CHARTWELL BOOKS, INC.** A division of **BOOK SALES, INC.**
110 Enterprise Avenue, Secaucus, New Jersey 07094
© 1981 Illustrations and text: Colour Library International Ltd., New Malden, Surrey, England.
Colour separations by FERCROM, Barcelona, Spain.
Display and text filmsetting by Focus Photoset & The Printed Word, London, England.
Printed by JISA-RIEUSSET, bound by EUROBINDER-Barcelona-Spain
ISBN 0-89009-426-8 Library of Congress Card No. 80-70183